RECKONING DAY

Thanks for your support!
Be inspired!
♡ Dawn

ALSO BY DAWN JAMISON

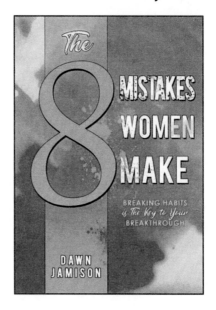

COMING IN 2019

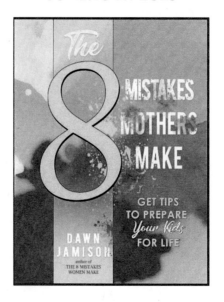

RECKONING DAY

#METOO *Stories That Inspire You*

DAWN JAMISON

PARENTAL WARNING ~
GRAPHIC CONTENT WARNING

This book may contain content of an adult nature. If you are easily offended, sensitive to abuse, or are under the age of 18, please take note of this advisory before reading. The stories within are intended for adults only and may include sexual content and violence. Reader discretion is advised.

Printed in the United States of America

Library of Congress Cataloging-in-Publication Data
Jamison, Dawn.

Library of Congress Control Number: 2018943167

ISBN: 0-9998512-0-9

ISBN-13: 978-0-9998512-0-3

First Edition.

This book is dedicated to all of the women who are not able to say Me Too and live in silence after enduring sexual harassment or violence. Your experiences were not in vain. Each of you serve as a symbol of strength and resilience to the world. May each reader be inspired by these women and their stories of truth.

"Stories have to be told or they die, and when they die, we can't remember who we are or why we're here."
-Author Sue Monk Kidd

CONTENTS

CHAPTER THREE: ACQUAINTANCE RAPE

CHAPTER FOUR: RELIGIOUS TIES

CHAPTER FIVE: A HOSTILE WORK ENVIRONMENT

CHAPTER SIX: ABUSE OF POWER

CHAPTER 7: MEN ARE SURVIVORS, TOO

CONCLUSION: WHAT DO WE DO NOW?

ABOUT THE BOOK

Reckoning Day was written to pour high-octane gasoline over the blazing fire we've witnessed through storytelling and the long-overdue #MeToo Movement. This historic, international dialogue about abuse has already resulted in important changes pertaining to women's rights, activism and justice. This movement is unlike anything we've ever seen in history. It has proved that there is great power in unity, power in raising our voices, power in empathy and power in storytelling.

Over the course of the past year, I have had dozens of in-depth interviews to capture the heartfelt stories of survivors from around the country and the world. Many of these have left me in tears thinking about the impact abuse has had on these and other survivors like them. This book is one of the first to be published post the 2017 #MeToo Movement that provides a historical account while sharing a compilation of abuse stories. It features 20 real stories of women and men who faced down abuse or harassment in a variety of arenas. Each one is important and metaphorically symbolizes millions more stories around the world that may still be secret and untold.

Last year's avalanche of stories from famous Hollywood celebrities re-introduced the world to this important movement. However, you won't find any Hollywood stories here. There is no fan base for the survivors in this book, and this isn't a memoir. Rather, *Reckoning Day* serves as a platform to learn about everyday survivors who have braved years of abuse and its harsh effects, and who are now ready to share their experiences. Some of the names have been changed to protect the survivors' identities.

These moving stories are part of the wave of broken silence that is currently rolling through society. Thousands of bold women and brave men are finding the strength and gumption to share their difficult experiences to help others along their journey of healing and protect others from victimization.

Thus, this book is not only for people who can personally relate to abuse, but it is for everyone: Men, women, gay, straight, young and old. Everyone <u>needs</u> to know the type of appalling realities that many victims face every day of their lives. As the title suggests, these stories hopefully will inspire you into action; inspire you to be a part of the solution in this epic fight against normalized abuse.

As a note of caution, these stories may also disgust, enrage, bother, shock or frighten you as you witness the things women have endured at the hands of some pretty barbaric men and women. Before you begin reading, I want to prepare you for the stories that contain raw descriptions of abuse.

So, why share abuse stories? Because these convincing accounts cover a wide range of abuse, yet they offer readers empathy, encouragement, relatability, and most importantly, shareable lessons to learn. I don't claim to be a sexual assault expert; however, as a journalist, I take my job seriously when it comes to sharing valuable information with the people who need it the most.

We need to have a broader conversation about the implications of misogyny, male privilege and abuse. We need to have a real conversation about why in 2018 some men treat women like their property, and more importantly, why the systems around abusers allow bad behavior to persist. We have to take a look at why abuse is so widespread and how it impacts both the victims and abusers on a mental and spiritual level.

As an outspoken women's advocate, I want to share stories that can provide fodder for further discussions, warnings and lessons themselves. On a deeper level, we need to consider how long-suffering abuse shows up in our communities. And instead of pushing these gruesome incidents to the back of our minds, we need to begin taking practical steps to provide safeguards and educational resources.

In this book you will find I use "#MeToo" to refer specifically to the 2017 Twitter phenomenon. In contrast, I use "Me Too" in a broader sense to describe the entire movement of change and its far-reaching results.

Additionally, the last chapter is a resource guide with domestic abuse hotlines and websites from around the country for those who live or work in abusive environments. Please share this information and resources with those in your own community. My prayer is that survivors be emboldened after reading these stories, and that all readers take time to will share the resources in this book with those in need.

Let's stay connected! If you want to share your story, please visit the *Reckoning Day* Facebook Fan Page,

DawnJamison.com, or tweet me at @IamDawnJamison. Don't forget to use #ReckoningDay on social media! This book is available in paperback and eBook and will soon be available on ACX as an audiobook. (TED Talks, I'm coming for you!) If you enjoy this book, the highest compliment you can give is passing it along to another amazing person who can benefit from reading it!

FOREWORD

"It's Time for Justice"

As a social worker, advocating for clients for social justice issues is not just a part of my career, it is also a part of my value system. As a woman of color, I am descended from a strong, resilient group of women who have endured hundreds of years of abuse. This abuse began at the hands of the white slave owners who repeatedly forced them into unwanted sexual acts and unwanted pregnancies.

Since then, abuse has been perpetrated upon women of color at the hands of employers, family members, and even significant others. But women of color are not the only women who've been subjected to abuse. Abuse knows no race, ethnicity, educational background or socioeconomic status. Abuse knows no bounds and can have a devastating and damaging impact upon those on the receiving end.

In America, a country that is supposed to be the leader of the free world, over the past year we have experienced the election of a man who has boasted about sexually harassing women. This man has unleashed the worst kind of hate and disrespect toward women that this country has ever seen! There have been countless media stories about women from public office, Hollywood celebrities, and more, who have come out and spoken up publicly about being sexually harassed and abused. But what about the women who cannot speak up for themselves? What about the women who are not public figures or celebrities? What about the everyday woman who feels like she has no voice?

In comes the #MeToo Movement. Founded more than 10 years ago by Tarana Burke, the #MeToo Movement encouraged women to speak out about sexual violence and harassment. It served as a pathway to healing for all women, but especially women of color in low-income communities, whose voices are often not heard. The movement was popularized after the hashtag was tweeted around Hollywood to support women who had come forward and encouraged other women to speak out about sexual harassment and violence.

But speaking out about sexual harassment and violence is more than just a hashtag and a movement. It has to be a way of life for this country and the world to keep our daughters safe from the devastating effects of abuse.

Burke explains it this way: "We need a complete cultural transformation if we are to eradicate sexual assault in our lifetime. This means we must build our families differently, engage our communities, and confront some of our long-held assumptions about ourselves."

Burke's sentiments are the catalyst for *Reckoning Day: #MeToo Stories That Inspire You.* This book is ahead of the curve, as the world has yet to see many books specifically addressing the movement, survivor stories, and much-needed resources for victims. Author Dawn Jamison uncovers everything from inspiring stories of brave survivors of child abuse to women who've endured harassment in the workplace. These stories were written to continue the dialogue about eradicating sexual harassment, violence, and all forms of abuse that are destroying our people, communities, and society as a whole. I applaud the courageous women and men who so selflessly tell their stories so that others may gain healing in their lives. Their individual stories shine a bright spotlight on the enormous impact abuse has had on our society.

This book is for survivors, abusers, political figures, professionals helping others to heal, and anyone else who is ready to transform our country and world into a safer, more loving place where all can thrive.

Reckoning Day will serve as a reminder to check our own behavior for signs that we are causing pain, abuse, or violence in the lives of others. It will surely provide support and encouragement to survivors who may want to tell their stories. *Reckoning Day* is relevant and timely in the current climate of unity among survivors as they raise their voices.

As a seasoned social worker who routinely investigates child abuse cases, I have seen first-hand how abuse destroys lives, causes shame and embarrassment, and leaves children vulnerable. I have seen first-hand how domestic abuse leaves women feeling low and unsupported. Abuse of any kind can spur symptoms associated with post-traumatic stress disorder and can cause victims to face low self-worth that can potentially lead to suicidal behavior and shatter families' lives.

It is time for us to take a stand and speak out against sexual harassment, violence, and abuse in a bolder way. Enough is enough! It's time to reclaim our communities with healing. It is time for women and girls everywhere to feel safer and loved. Today is our Reckoning Day!

— DR. DAPHNE L. KING

Dr. King is Co-Founder of Quit for Passion with Dawn Jamison. She is also a college professor, an entrepreneur, and a champion for social justice. She earned her doctorate in Social Work at Argosy University and has worked in the field for over 20 years. She is the author of Love Heals All Wounds, The Warrington Clan: Love's Whirlwind, and is a co-author of Kingdom Upgrade: A Next Level Shift.

INTRODUCTION

"There is a movement happening. There is a groundswell of passion and conviction rising among women and men."
-Chelsea Handler

Reckoning Day is here! The 2017 #MeToo Movement marked the era of silence breakers and revolutionary social change regarding the way women are treated behind closed doors (and perhaps publicly too). It ushered in a new era where notorious sexual predators finally began facing justice for longtime abuse. This book aims to continue this critical domestic and international discussion by women who have collectively raised their voices to say "Enough!" Now we're witnessing an extraordinary time of solidarity among survivors of abuse and sexual violence.

For the first time, we're seeing repercussions from power brokers, bad press about men's grotesque behavior, and resignations and firings of notable men in entertainment, media, and sports industries. We've seen millions of empowered women (and men) publicly share their stories in a bolder way. Women have immobilized and unified for marches, protests and organized efforts in the name of ending sexual violence.

The Trump Effect

It's painful to admit, but I partially credit President Donald Trump for this spectacular eruption of enthusiasm among women who have thrust the #MeToo Movement into the limelight. "The Trump Effect" has been characterized a few different ways, but one of the most popular definitions is the broad resistance to his presidency and the action that has spurred millions of women to protest, get politically active and run for office. Trump's reckless sexual misconduct with scores of women, including porn stars and Playboy bunnies, has signaled a new transformational period for women.

The Trump Effect is responsible for spurring the Women's March on Washington just one day after Trump took office. According to news reports, the women's march drew between three million and five million marchers, and it was the largest one-day protest on record in U.S. history. And the marches didn't stop there. Women and men in Paris, Nairobi, Berlin, Cape Town, Sydney and London hosted "sister marches" in protest of Trump.

Because Trump has supported anti-abortion organizations and undone health care laws that provide contraception for women, many have lashed out. There are numerous public social media campaigns, and many women have used their fund-raising dollars to speak for them.

Political and civic activism is up among women across the country. For instance, Cecile Richards, president of Planned Parenthood, said the organization has gained more than one million new supporters since Trump was elected last year. In a surprising twist, Trump's lewd actions, sexist remarks, and the allegations of sexual assault against him have helped stir up women everywhere.

Not to mention the record number of women around the nation, such as Christine Lui Chen of New Jersey, Mary Barzee Flores of Florida, and Dana Nessel of Michigan, who openly credit Trump's victory for their motivation to run for office. This news is music to my ears, despite all of this talk about harassment and sexism.

Regrettably, sexual violence against women is not a new topic. This has likely been going on in our homes, the workplace, schools, our communities and beyond, since the dawn of time. Abuse of power, molestation, stalking, rape, sexual assault, and slavery, are all harsh realities that many women live with every day.

In fact, at this very moment, there are new acts of violence taking place and new survivors who desperately need support. However, many parents, siblings, family members, co-workers, teammates, neighbors and the like choose to turn a blind eye to such horrific abuse. It seems that our numb society spends more time minimizing harassment than finding real solutions for the widespread problem. As a woman who barely escaped a sexually violent situation myself, I've learned that sexual assault is more often about power and control than it is about sex. This misuse of power, sexual aggression and misconduct is a familiar theme in Hollywood, too.

In October of 2017, a massive wave of celebrity interrupters, such as Alyssa Milano, Gabrielle Union, Reese Witherspoon, and Lupita Nyong'o, began to boldly speak out about well-known predators in the entertainment industry, such as film director Harvey Weinstein. The list of famed predators has expanded to include Tavis Smiley, Senator Al Franken, James Franco, Matt Lauer, Russell Simmons and Charlie Rose.

Because of them, Twitter, one of the fastest growing social media platforms in the world, became a popular place for women connect. Thanks to Milano, survivors started sharing their disgust about sexual harassment and abuse in mid-October. Her single tweet, shown below, about speaking out, unlatched a tweet storm. Inside of 48 hours there were more than 1.5 million response tweets and more than 13.5 million posts across social media platforms.

In the infamous tweet, Milano referenced the "Me Too" Movement that had been launched over 10 years prior by a social justice activist from Philadelphia.

The Woman Who Started It All

Many people have heard about Weinstein and the prominent role that Hollywood celebs have played. However, less known is that in 2006 Tarana Burke had begun a local "Me Too" campaign when she worked with young abuse survivors in her hometown. She began using "empowerment through empathy" as a tool of support for them.

Burke, who is a survivor of childhood sexual abuse, said the #MeToo Movement actually began because she was

unsuccessful at finding resources for survivors in her community. Subsequently, she launched her company, Just Be Inc. in 2006, which was inspired by other women's survival stories and focused on empowering young women. Burke is the important match to this wildfire we've seen arise against sexual abuse. Burke's early vision for and as a survivor have played a critical role in the #MeToo Movement.

Credit: Just Be Inc.

She, along with other women's rights activists, laid the movement foundation, even though it wouldn't become an international phenomenon until over a decade later.

Burke has been quoted as saying that "Me Too" was initially all about sexual violence survivors relating to other survivors. Burke believes the movement is much bigger than her, bigger than Weinstein, and is more about the ramped acceptance of sexual violence and abuse.

"For every Harvey Weinstein, there are 100,000 more folks around us every day," Burke said in a 2017 MTV interview. "We need to look at our neighbors, uncles, coaches, priests and pastors. Predators are everywhere, and they are representative of a larger problem."

Since then, Burke has shared her story on the national stage and began working with celebrities and organizations around the country to get her message out. She wants more conversation and action around sexual violence against women.

During an October 2017 Good Morning America interview, Milano emphasized how prevalent sexual assault is against women and how she hopes more women raise their voices against sexist practices.

"This happens everywhere; it's not just actresses ... it's women just walking down the street," Milano explained passionately. "I've been harassed so many times that I can't count [the instances]."

Milano said she planned to collaborate with Burke and [would] do everything she can to make a real impact on gender equality.

"The MeToo Campaign has put the focus back on the victims. It enables us to say, 'No More!'" In the interview, Milano exclaimed: "We're not going to put up with this anymore! We're going to be vocal about this until it stops."

Burke, who has publicly praised Milano for attracting national attention with the MeToo hashtag, has explained: "'Me Too' can be both a whole conversation or just a conversation starter." She has said that just uttering those words can take the place of explaining a whole traumatic story.

Burke also said it's like saying, "I get it. I feel you," and can create an instant connection with other survivors.

"One of the main things that I felt as a young survivor is I felt alone," Burke told MTV about her abuse. "It was my secret shame. There was no way to talk about it because I was a child."

She went on to say: "As I child, I felt like I broke all of the rules. As children, you hear your parents say, 'Don't let anybody touch your private parts,' or, 'Don't walk away with strangers.' So, you feel like, oh my God, I broke these rules."

In her early years of working on the campaign, Burke could see how widespread abuse was after meeting survivors at training and speaking engagements. She was quoted saying: "[I found that] survivors empathized with my situation and helped me to feel like I wasn't alone."

Burke has emphasized the comforting way the #MeToo Movement helps to erase guilt and shame associated with abuse.

"People are ashamed to have these conversations. Shame is debilitating, but empathy stomps out shame," she said of the way survivors have come together for support. "[The movement] takes away the stigma of talking about this … And we need people who are not survivors to stand up."

Like Burke, I have always felt compelled to support survivors by volunteering at women's shelters, organizing food drives, and organizing donation drives in the past. This has especially been important because of the way domestic abuse and harassment have impacted me personally.

As the fallout from the #MeToo Movement developed, I watched with the rest of the world, cheering on the survivors who, one-by-one, used their voices to take down notorious sexual predators. But as the Hollywood buzz around the

#MeToo revelations grew, everyday women also began breaking the silence about their abuse experiences.

The movement was in the hearts and minds of women around the world, and many of us couldn't help but reflect on our own families and personal experiences. I believe in one way or another, we've all been touched by abuse at close range.

Me Too

In less than five minutes flat, I found myself trapped under a guy after our first date. In retrospect, I never did see anyone else inside his family's house before I found myself pinned to the carpeted floor. It felt as if a side embrace had gone from zero to 100 as he pulled at my pants and went for my neck in a Dracula kind of way. It's truly a mystery just how this seemingly nice teenager morphed into a sexually-charged predator in the blink of an eye! My repeated plea to "Get off" didn't seem to mean much to him, but I quickly discovered that my closed fist and my elbow proved to be two very effective tools.

I morphed into Flo-Jo as I made a mad dash out the side door and toward my mom's Grand Am. Tears welled up in my eyes and my heart raced a million miles a minute.

This was my earliest memory of sexual assault, which occurred during my junior year of high school shortly after I started driving. I had met the "nice" guy at the mall the month prior and had an innocent date at a movie theater in my hometown. When the lackluster movie was over, he explained that his mom couldn't pick him up and asked if I could drop him off. I hesitated since we'd just met and I had my mother's car, but I obliged nonetheless. Looking back, he was trying to lure me in by reassuring me that his family was home. And with that, I figured coming inside a few minutes wouldn't hurt since his "family was home."

After the assault, I processed the significance of that night and how it was and could have been even more of a pivotal moment in my life. I never heard from the ass hole again, and I, like many women in these predicaments, never bothered to tell anyone. It is just one of many instances I can effortlessly rattle off where I've felt threatened or have been in a dangerous predicament over the past 20 years.

But that day marked a shift in my awareness of men and the physical threat they posed. In the following weeks after the assault, I kept blaming myself for even ending up in a sticky situation. I kept replaying the tape about how I should've heard the insincerity in his voice and looked for danger signs. (Even almost-victims are conditioned to blame themselves before they blame their perpetrators.)

The topic of harassment and abuse got me thinking about my grandmother Yvonne and my deceased grandfather, Dan. Grandma was the first woman to come to mind because at age 17, she was the only woman I knew who had faced abuse. It was common knowledge in my family that Grandpa Dan had physically and emotionally abused her in front of their seven children throughout their 12-year relationship.

Even decades after their relationship ended, I wondered about the abuse that had a profound impact on my dad, his siblings, and ultimately, on me. After my assault, I had reluctantly become more aware of the way men treated the women around me. And I had also come to notice the dearth of healthy marriages around me. Even at my young age, I recalled countless stories of how Grandpa Dan had "beat the hell out of Grandma."

I was curious why Grandma stayed in her common-law marriage for as long as she had, and why she subjected herself and her young children to such treatment for so long. I asked about the abuse at the hands of my absent grandfather I barely knew — especially since I knew Grandpa Dan was barely half her size and shorter than her. Dan Hudson, like Grandma, never graduated from high school and could barely write his own name. And ironically, despite the abuse Grandma endured, she was single-handedly responsible for helping Grandpa learn how to read. This known drunk and womanizer almost never financially provided for her, yet somehow, he owned all of the control in their relationship.

When I did get around to asking Grandma about the whole thing, her answer was simple. She said: "I was afraid of him all of those years, and he used my fear to his advantage. I remember being deathly afraid of Dan giving me a black eye, so I would just cover my face with my arms when his temper showed up. And when we would eat dinner as a family, he would sit with his gun in his lap and it was very intimidating."

With regret in her voice, Grandma Yvonne, who is now 92, recounted the way my father and his siblings would sob when Grandpa Dan got violent. I asked her about the root of his violence and she pointed to his constant state of drunkenness and his foul behavior.

"Your grandfather was just a mean man," she explained. "He had no reservation of slapping me dead in the face on any given day. Anywhere I would go, he would accuse me of seeing another man."

"I ain't been nowhere," Grandma explained in slang. "Yet, he would come home after being gone for days, cussing and calling me a 'black so-and-so.'"

Recounting their past blow-ups, Grandma said the idea of her seeing another man was just a silly concept, particularly because she was pregnant throughout much of their relationship and had several mouths to feed at home. They were raising their family in poverty in the country city of White Cloud, Michigan.

"Looking back, your grandpa just wanted to feel like the man, and his way of doing that was to put me down," Grandma said. "He would tell me, 'Shut up and sit down,' and expected me not to talk back. As if I was his child."

With certainty in her voice, Grandma said if she had had someone in her life to help build her confidence and straighten out her wrong thinking, she wouldn't have suffered through her relationships as much as she did. But her mom, great-grandma Delores, had abandoned her children at an early age, so Grandma never had a parent in her life to provide direction on parenting and critical life decisions.

Grandma Yvonne had spent most of her working years in farm fields, or as a housekeeper. "Back in those days," she said, "I was so glad to have a man and I thought to stay with him was the right thing to do. In my mind, I felt like I was so in love with him. But nobody told me that's not what love is about. Even though I would cry, he would promise he'd never do it again and I believed him every time."

Finally, Grandma built up enough gumption to flee her abuser in the darkness of night. A close friend literally drove her getaway car as my grandfather slept, blacked out from a night of heavy drinking. After nearly 12 years of abuse, Grandma apparently had enough. She never looked back.

The abuse Grandma Yvonne endured would have a permanent impact on the next two generations of the Hudson family. My family never learned what a healthy marriage looked like; thus, some of the relatives also found themselves in abusive relationships, while others seemed to replicate the abusive behavior they saw as children. The abuse Grandma endured impacted her children deeply on many levels. And as her grandchild, I feel those wounds in a very real way even now. But, I know many other families can say the same. I really don't think society fully grasps all of the ways that domestic and sexual abuse show up.

Sisters in the Struggle

My stories are not special. Each of us has a story, some deeper and more painful than others. No matter what type of abuse women have endured, they have found a way to connect, with compassion as the common thread. What I know for sure is that two little words, "Me Too," have connected tens of thousands of women and men around the world. Over the past year, this resilient community of survivors have shared heartfelt stories, created support groups, and encouraged one another through the power of empathy.

As a journalist, storytelling is the most powerful tool at my fingertips. Stories motivate, challenge, educate and help us to understand the gravity of major problems like abuse. Whether they come in the form of top news stories, Facebook posts, or juicy gossip, stories like these are the way we emotionally connect with each other. So many of us have been impacted by abuse on a personal level that we all can relate to stories of trials and triumph like the ones shared in this book.

One-by-one, *Reckoning Day* allows readers to take in powerful stories that are symbolic of millions more. Some details are tough to swallow; however, these stories aren't intended to create a melodramatic or depressing effect. Rather, I'm continuing a conversation about the impact of abuse and urging readers to be a part of the solution. Hopefully, everyone is inspired to support other survivors, share stories in a constructive spirit, begin healing, and find ways to positively impact their communities.

So, how has the #MeToo Movement impacted you? Have you been challenged by the new conversations and revelations that have resulted? For me, I was empowered to share meaningful stories as well as my own.

I've witnessed the way this movement has the power to move each of us in small and big ways. Above all, understand that no matter what you've been through or are going through now, you're not alone. Everywhere I go, I meet women who share experiences just like these. And, perhaps, like yours.

If you are an abuser survivor, may these stories comfort you and serve as a glimmer of hope. Each featured survivor has persevered to get to a better place in their life. As you read each story, remember that each of us can be a positive ray of light for survivors in our lives.

CHAPTER ONE

Spousal Abuse

"We have been siloed off from each other. We're finally hearing each other, and seeing each other, and now locking arms in solidarity." -Reese Witherspoon

Spousal abuse can result when one person in an intimate relationship or marriage has control over the other. According to the Center for Disease Control, nearly 10 million women and men face spousal abuse every year. Whether it's the neighbors or family members reporting abuse to authorities, marital or relationship abuse can be a colossal secret that rips couples and families apart.

Battered spouses face emotional, psychological, physical and sexual abuse. Some abuse survivors I interviewed say they stayed in their toxic relationships because of their children together. Some battered women and men often stay to serve as a buffer to protect their children from harm. Understandably, some survivors opt for the road of least resistance and continue taking the blows from their abuser rather than face unpredictable anger. Meanwhile, others fear that if they flee their abusive relationship without their children, they run the risk of losing custody or contact with them.

In some instances, well-meaning victims believe their abusive spouse is a "good person," and they are in denial of the gravity of abuse impacting themselves and their children. They sometimes go to great lengths to hide family abuse or even defend their abusive spouses because they are blinded by their love for the abuser.

Some survivors I interviewed told me their abusers often over-emphasized how important they were in their lives. Other survivors reported that their husbands and boyfriends went to great pains to manipulate them and make them feel as if they "deserved" the abuse. Still others said they were "brainwashed" to believe they were "worthless" and that "no one else would want them." These perpetual emotional beatings can often lead to low self-esteem and depression.

Domestic Violence Statistics

1/3 Women have been physically abused	**1/4** Men have been physically abused	**20,800** On a typical day, domestic violence hotlines are called 20,800 times
15% Domestic violence accounts for 15% of all violent crime	**500%** A gun in a domestic violence situation increases the risk of homicide by 500%	**19%** 19% of all domestic violence involves a weapon

National Coalition Against Domestic Violence

***

Lynda

"I sometimes wonder how I even got mixed up in domestic violence because I never saw any of that growing up with my parents," Lynda Mines began. "My first husband was so possessive that sometimes he would show up at my job at the VA just to make sure I was there."

As if it happened yesterday, Lynda vividly remembers the afternoon she jumped from the second-story window of her suburban home to escape her first abusive husband. By the time her second abusive husband came into her life, she had grown braver and wiser about warning signs.

Lynda's first husband, William, was a well-known Detroit-area barber and business owner who was 20 years her senior. He was known for his voice and often sang locally with the likes of the superstar gospel group, The Clark Sisters.

"If William ever saw a man make a pass at me, he would beat me and lock me up," said Lynda, who was only 23 at the time. "When I was pregnant with our daughter, he would beat me. And he continued to lock me up at our house so that I couldn't get out."

Despite the harsh realities Lynda faced, her life looked idealistic from the outside. At the time, she drove a luxury car and lived in a large home in a gated suburban community. At one point she and William even had a maid and servants working in their home.

"But one day after he beat me, I remember pushing the second-story window open and just jumping," said Lynda as she reminisced about the day she safely leaped to her freedom. "Only God saved me that day. It was hard, but I had to make a choice to leave my young daughter behind as she napped."

After her landing, Lynda bolted as fast as she could to the nearby clubhouse in her subdivision. Desperate, she went to the bathroom to wipe her bruised face and call the police. When they arrived, they transported Lynda to the nearby hospital for a thorough examination. She believed her husband and parents would look after her daughter in her absence.

"I ended up in a women's shelter because I didn't want my family to immediately know what was happening" said Lynda. "The sad part is, I ended up going back to him. After that, I still dealt with the same beatings, and he was telling lies to our family."

Since the domestic abuse persisted, Lynda plotted another escape, only this time she planned to take her daughter with her. She stashed away money for her great escape, and also borrowed some from her supportive parents.

"The second time I left him was in 1996, when my daughter and I took a Greyhound bus all the way to sunny Orlando," Lynda said. "I got a job as a medical assistant and put my daughter in nearby daycare. I felt so much relief and called my parents to let them know we were doing all right."

After about six months of peaceful living in Florida, Lynda received news that her godmother had passed away. So, she and her daughter went back to Michigan for the funeral, but soon after, Lynda's beloved mother died as well.

"Unfortunately, William and I had reconciled again," Lynda recalled about her on again, off again relationship with her husband. "Only this time he moved to Florida with us. Together we got a house and were living in Treasure Island."

Lynda says it wasn't long before William began the physical and emotional abuse again. "So, for an entire month, I was contemplating killing him after I kept waking up with a gun to my head," she said, choking up. "I didn't even know who I was because he was beating and kicking me so badly."

Abruptly, Lynda received a divinely-ordered phone call from her sister-in-law, who lived in Detroit. The call likely saved her life. Lynda remembered being surprised because she wasn't clear how her distant sister-in-law even got her number.

"She called saying, 'I have been thinking about you and I just called to say don't let my brother make you lose your mind!'"

Lynda recalled the significance of the phone call because her sister-in-law had previously served time in prison for shooting her former boyfriend. "I remember the day she called clearly," Lynda said, "because I just started packing up my daughter's stuff to go to a shelter in St. Petersburg." Lynda remembers fleeing with a measly $100 to her name. Thanks to the adopt-a-family program at her shelter, her daughter was able to enjoy a few presents under their Christmas tree.

"Looking back, I think I stayed as long as I had because our relationship reminded me of my childhood," Lynda admitted. "I thought William was a man of God and I loved the way we would regularly go to church together."

Lynda's daughter was eight years old the last time the three of them were together. Around this time, Lynda ended up moving back to the Detroit area.

"I had unsuccessfully tried to serve William with divorce papers so many times," she said about her 10-year marriage. "And my soon-to-be future husband accompanied me to the law office to sign the paperwork."

At age 31, Lynda married for the second time and thought that her future looked bright. Her new husband, Donald, was a longtime Detroit police officer who had been married twice. She would soon learn that the man she fell in love with was also a closet alcoholic.

"I would also learn that he was the same devil as my first husband, but in a different package this time," she said. "It started with mental abuse and then he started getting physical with me."

After giving birth to her second daughter, Lynda recalled coming home one birthday and learning that her step-son had moved into their family home. Donald forcefully lashed out at her with the news, saying that, "You'll just have to deal with it," without her input.

"One day my husband accidentally left his cell phone at home when I discovered that he had been cheating on me," said Lynda. She also said that Donald had recently broken her arm in a verbal disagreement. "Between the abuse and the cheating, I decided I wanted a divorce."

When Lynda told the leaders and members of her church about the abuse and her decision to file for divorce, she said it felt like everyone was against her.

"In my first marriage, I was silenced because I was ashamed of myself and the abuse," she explained. "But this time, when I shared my marital struggles, it still felt like I was in the battle all by myself."

Her husband put up a bitter fight for custody of their daughter, and at one point, Lynda temporarily lost custody because of Donald's false allegations that she was an unfit mother.

"I felt like I was losing my mind. When I attended a church revival, it had a major impact on me and gave me hope to fight on," Lynda said.

Lynda started using her marital experiences to help other men and women in difficult relationships. Consumed by her legal and emotional battles, Lynda said she had forgotten about self-care, and that she was beautiful. She decided to create a vision board with encouraging messages. Her vision board included biblical scripture and affirmations, like: "I am royal" and "I am healed."

"I got my mind off of myself and started helping other women with their situations," she said after her second divorce was final. The two-sided vision board she created also had a 12-step process on how to bring yourself back to who you once were.

Today, Lynda is self-employed and a proud new grandmother. She tells her survivor story in local speeches because she firmly believes it can help inspire others to be prosperous and to heal after abuse.

"One day, I said that I would tell my story, and I am finally getting the chance," Lynda said joyfully. "My mess is my message."

Her Advice: "Don't put your husband on a pedestal. Never lose who you are and never quit a job because a man tells you that he'll take care of you."

***

Dana

For nearly 17 years, Dana Carter lived with a nightmare — her abusive ex-husband, Terrell. With their four young children in tow, the family reluctantly moved in and out of approximately 10 homeless shelters around Missouri and Kansas over the years. Unfortunately, Terrell's erratic behavior was the reason the family frequently got kicked out of shelters.

"At the beginning of our relationship, I believed everything he told me," Dana explained. "But it was a whirlwind being married to that man. I began to notice that Terrell was very different in public with his charm, but then he would be yelling at me for hours in private."

Dana, who is from New Jersey, was two years younger than Terrell when they married in 2002. She perceived him as a very caring person in the early years, but later began to see his true colors.

"We were homeless so many times, and it was hard because he isolated me from my entire family," she said. "Unfortunately, I had total dependence on Terrell so I stayed with him."

Dana reminisced about happily staying in the Rose Brooks Center in Kansas City, Missouri at the time when Oprah

Winfrey's Angel Network gave the shelter $1 million dollars for expansion and renovations.

"After Oprah's donation, that was by far the nicest and most comfortable shelter we had stayed in," she recalled. "Our room key looked like a hotel key. The shelter even added a wing where residents could bring their pets. Most people who flee a bad situation typically leave their beloved pets behind."

Dana's two-word description for her ex-husband was "manipulative and controlling." She recalled the laundry list of rules he created for her, including no speaking in church, no wearing nail polish — and sometimes, due to his lack of a job, no food.

Dana recalled Terrell's cruelty. "If I looked people in the face, then my husband would yell at me. At times, he would force me to eat food, and other times he would withhold food from our kids so we could eat food they could not have. There were times when he wouldn't even allow me to feed our kids, so I would sneak food to them when I could."

Dana recalls how Terrell threatened to kill her on several occasions, and even picked her up during his rages and dropped her on the floor. He threatened to call Child Protective Services on her, and often used drugs to self-medicate.

'We almost got our children taken away from us," she admitted tearfully. "They were definitely affected by the abuse. At times, Terrell would make them stand perfectly in line in order of ages when we were shopping in public."

After the toxic marriage ended, Dana spent extra time explaining to their children that the relationship was not ideally how marriage should be.

"Terrell would tell me, 'You won't have nothing without me,' after he ruined my credit and my rental history," said Dana. She added that her children don't have a relationship with their dad anymore. "Back then, I just wanted him to be nice to me. Because when you go through this you feel very alone, and as if you have no voice. My faith in God kept me going."

Dana struggled with her weight throughout her life and said Terrell would strategically leverage the weakness to control her with food.

"He would always say hurtful things like, 'You are so fat and nobody else will want you,'" she recalled.

Dana later found out that Terrell had fathered other children during their marriage. She also discovered that her ex-husband's family had a frightening history of incest and abuse. She learned that Terrell's mother had even tried to abort her son because he was unwanted and unloved.

"His family was very unsafe for my kids. And his mother wanted nothing to do with our children." Dana said. "Later on, Terrell admitted that he had shot a woman and proudly caused the ex-girlfriend to have a limp because of the abuse."

Now 52-year-old Dana is a successful business owner and a mentor to battered and homeless women. Since her divorce she has begun visiting shelters around her community to give speeches on how to get out of abusive relationships.

Her ministry, Precious Pearls, helps women and children who are or have been domestically abused.

Her Advice: "You deserve more than an abusive relationship. Abuse is not love. Be cognizant when your mate tries to isolate you. Remember to listen to your family. You are precious and you deserve to treated that way."

***

Tia

Tia McElroy tearfully reflected on the 19 traumatic years of abuse she and their three children endured at the hands of her ex-husband, Martin. The Western Michigan University sweethearts dated for four or five years and married in 1993. Shortly after marrying, their relationship took a turn for the worse.

"Although Martin never physically abused me before we married," said Tia, now 49. "I did remember him sharing stories about fighting people, like his sports teammates, but that was about it."

Tia recalled the way her ex-husband had complete control of their bank account. Just a few months after their wedding she had used the couple's checkbook to purchase a new bedspread for their room. Once Martin saw the bedding that Tia had purchased without permission, he took a pillow and began violently hitting his pregnant wife with it.

"Early in our marriage, my husband had dragged me down the hallway of our apartment building by my hair," Tia said. He had left their infant sitting alone in their apartment. "One of our neighbors called the police. But, instead of leaving him, we ended up getting back together and having two more kids."

As the abuse escalated, Martin punched holes in the walls of their home, and at one point, ripped the door off of the hinges.

"Martin threw piping-hot oatmeal on me in front of our kids, who were just 11, 8 and 7 at the time," said Tia, who admitted she saw her own father be abusive toward her mother. "I was in shock, but I just thought this was my cross to bear."

Amazingly, Tia says no one outside of her immediate family knew about her abuse or the increasingly abusive behavior toward their children. Because her husband was a well-known businessman in their community, she preferred to kept it secret.

When Tia spent time with her girlfriends, she said, "All of my conversations centered heavily around my kids."

As the abuse toward their children intensified, there were a number of times when Tia feared she and Martin would lose custody of their three children. She described Martin's discipline as way overboard. "He seemed to spank my son harder than our two girls. And it seemed like every little thing resulted in a beating. At times, he treated my son like a man. My son's little butt was bruised until it was black."

Whenever Tia considered telling someone about her abuse, she would be overwhelmed with a feeling of betrayal.

She was struck by the fact that her mother-in-law never attempted to come to her rescue, even after knowing about her son's dangerous behavior. And when Tia confided to her mother-in-law about the child abuse, her response was, "Well, we all beat our kids."

"Over time, I could feel the abuse taking a toll on my health," Tia admitted. "There were days that I couldn't even get out of bed. And other times, I suffered from anxiety and my heart raced."

Tia says the threats and abuse left her feeling powerless and alone. She particularly struggled with the harsh punishments that her kids endured.

"Toward the end of our marriage, he purchased a handgun and I just knew that he was going to blow my head off," Tia recalled. "My weight was the under-current of our unhappy marriage. He couldn't stand me because my weight would fluctuate."

Tia says through the years, God put people in her life for different reasons. She secretly began seeing a therapist regularly to help her cope with the growing abuse.

"I started seeing her in 2010 and it took me a whole year before I had the courage to leave him," Tia admitted. "I saw her for five years because I did not want my daughter to fall into the same unhealthy pattern. And I didn't want my son to become abusive."

After she filed for divorce, Tia's therapist finally helped her realize that Martin "would never be the man she wanted him to be." Tia began to bring her three children to therapy sessions, too.

Now, Tia and her grown children are in a much better place emotionally. Tia, who works as a speech pathologist, says that when she sees Martin because of their children, they are cordial to each other.

Her Advice: "Stay in the word. Strengthening my relationship with God and staying in the word changed my attitude about my ex-husband. At first, I wanted him to burn in hell, and now I don't feel like that anymore."

The Last Word

Domestic violence can happen to anyone. However, statistics show that in the U.S., women between the ages of 16 and 24 are three times more likely to be domestic violence victims. When it comes to domestic violence, most people ask only one question: "Why do women stay?" They fail to realize that many battered women and men do not perceive themselves as abuse victims.

Moreover, one major problem is that survivors don't typically know how to identify the signs of abuse. Many are just accustomed to coping and hiding the toxic cycle from loved ones. Here are the three phases of domestic abuse, which are illustrated below. These examples come from Community Beyond Violence, a California-based organization dedicated to reducing violence.

The Cycle of Abuse

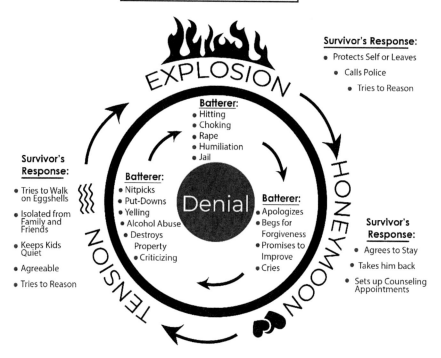

Survivor's Response:
- Protects Self or Leaves
  - Calls Police
    - Tries to Reason

Batterer:
- Hitting
- Choking
- Rape
- Humiliation
- Jail

Survivor's Response:
- Tries to Walk on Eggshells
- Isolated from Family and Friends
- Keeps Kids Quiet
- Agreeable
- Tries to Reason

Batterer:
- Nitpicks
- Put-Downs
- Yelling
- Alcohol Abuse
- Destroys Property
- Criticizing

Denial

Batterer:
- Apologizes
- Begs for Forgiveness
- Promises to Improve
- Cries

Survivor's Response:
- Agrees to Stay
- Takes him back
- Sets up Counseling Appointments

EXPLOSION

TENSION

HONEYMOON

#1 The Honeymoon Phase: The abuser seduces and charms the victim. This is the stage where the victim "falls deeply in love" and often feels like they've known the abuser for much longer than they have.

#2 The Tension Phase: In this phase, early signs may appear but are often dismissed as "little things." The abuser tries to control and isolate the victim from family and friends. In this phase, the victim tries not to make the abuser angry and tends to "walk on eggshells."

#3 The Explosion Phase: The abuser often makes physical threats, or slaps or beats the victim in this phase. If the abuse is only emotional or verbal, it can lead to physical abuse. The abuse will intensify and the frequency may increase, too.

The domestic abuse cycle begins again with the first phase and often with "The Apology." This consuming process can deplete self-esteem and emotionally drain the victim. It's commonly known as the stage when "the one you fell in love with" shows back up as the sweetest person in the world. In this phase, the apology serves as the "hook" that keeps victims stuck in the continuous and toxic cycle.

The ability to identify these phases and sharing this cycle could potentially save lives. A hefty list of resources can be found in the last chapter.

CHAPTER TWO

Child Abuse

"We all deserve to have our stories told."
— Kerry Washington

Since the #MeToo Movement broke last year, some survivors of childhood abuse say it triggered old feelings and bad memories. In this chapter, survivors discuss their experiences with molestation and child abuse. Amid all of the chatter about abuse, it's difficult for some who were abused as children to revisit their dark and traumatic past. As a result of childhood abuse, some survivors face isolation, psychological problems, cutting, hospitalizations, alcoholism, promiscuity, imprisonment and suicide attempts.

According to Childhelp.org, there are a staggering 3.6 million reports of child abuse made each year in the U.S. This translates into one child abuse report every 10 seconds! In the graphic below, you can see that the common child abuse categories include physical, sexual, emotional and neglect. More specifically, commonly reported cases also include inappropriate touching, visible bruising, exposure to pornography, online predatory reports and non-consensual sex.

According to the Rape, Abuse & Incest National Network (RAINN), one in nine girls and one in 53 boys in the U.S. will experience sexual abuse or assault before age 18. RAINN also reports that 93% of child sexual assault victims know the perpetrator. This means that grandfathers, neighbors, aunts, uncles, step-dads, cousins and even teachers are examples of people who may be too close for comfort with children.

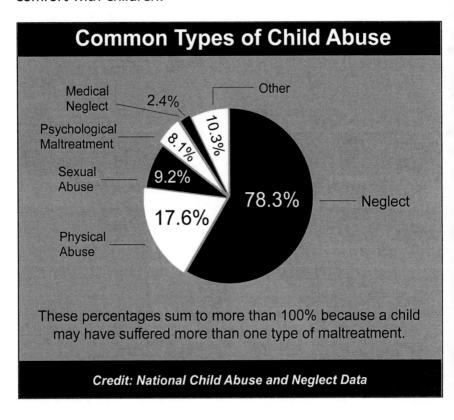

Common Types of Child Abuse

Medical Neglect — 2.4%
Other
Psychological Maltreatment — 8.1%
10.3%
Sexual Abuse — 9.2%
78.3% — Neglect
17.6%
Physical Abuse

These percentages sum to more than 100% because a child may have suffered more than one type of maltreatment.

Credit: National Child Abuse and Neglect Data

A Difficult Road

Many survivors of child abuse find it challenging to come out of such traumatic experiences with a healthy sense of self. These experiences can have a devastating impact on the life and maturation of a child and can continue to impact the survivor throughout his or her life. Research has shown that abuse affects brain development and the hormonal system. It can even cause sexually transmitted diseases and dysfunction in abused children. Many of these children have been brainwashed and conditioned to believe that the abuse was their fault.

Stamping out child abuse in this country is urgently important. Dismal statistics from the Child Welfare Information Gateway show that about 30% of abused children grow up to be abusers themselves. Moreover, statistics show that a high number of both female and male inmates admit being abused as children. Thus, acknowledging past trauma can help adults identify unhealthy patterns that show up down the road. Having a greater sense of awareness and acknowledgment of past abuse can be critically important in the healing process. Therapy support can help provide context to adult survivors.

***

Kate

Of all the survivors interviewed for *Reckoning Day,* Kate Romero's story is by far the most disturbing. She describes the powerful manner in which the #MeToo Movement has impacted her.

"I felt like I was released from a prison when the #MeToo Movement broke," Kate said happily. "At age 61, People are finally listening, and more importantly, believing me."

The Detroit native vividly reflects on the way her mentally ill mother regularly offered Kate up as a sexual sacrifice to her mom's pedophile boyfriend.

"My life was just a horrible, horrible existence," Kate began as she shared story after shocking story about living in poverty. "I was one of six kids living in the ghetto and each of us had a different father. So, I felt like none of us were really related or connected to each other. It felt like I was living with strangers who never became family."

Kate firmly believes her mother was a psychopath and likely suffered from schizophrenia, although she had never been formally diagnosed by a doctor. Kate's dad worked as an electrician and was often away for days at a time. Shortly after Kate was born, her mother gave her up to a family she had just met while her dad was away on a work assignment.

"When my dad returned, he realized that my mom had given me away to strangers," Kate explained. "So, he fought for custody and eventually brought me home again to live with them. However, just three weeks later, my dad died of a massive heart attack."

Thus, Kate landed back in her family's cramped apartment that was overrun by cockroaches. The family moved frequently because they were often evicted from apartments in cities and states all over the country.

"Everyone in my family harmed me in some way and [my mom] didn't do anything about it," Kate recalled. "In fact, she even encouraged the bad treatment. If [my siblings] were nice to me, they would have hell to pay with my mom."

Her mother had a high-risk pregnancy when Kate was 4-years-old, which meant she was unable to continue having sex with her live-in boyfriend, Rocky. Kate recalled that Rocky was drunk most of the time and her mom took care of him, along with her six stair-step children.

"Every day with my family was like a thousand fists against my soul," Kate said. "My brainwashed siblings were like a cult who only believed in violence and hate."

Kate's mom used a variety of tactics to harm her, including, beatings, over-feedings, and starvation. Kate ran away 13 times, but because her mom would not get her deceased father's pension if Kate did not live under her roof, Kate was always brought back by police.

"When I was four, my mom gave me over to Rocky as a sex toy," Kate said. "He would give me whiskey, give me nickels to take off my clothes. He would roughly bathe me in the bathtub full of water and pull me under by my genitals until I nearly drowned. He would then carry me like a football dripping wet to the living room where he would lay me across the arm of the sofa and sodomize me. I had blisters on my stomach from the sofa when I would wake up later with my clothes on inside out."

Kate was kept out of school until the age of 7 and on her very first day of school, she told her teacher that she was being sexually abused at home.

"But my teacher proceeded to call me 'a terrible child' and [said] that no one would do those things to their own family member. She told my mom about what I said," Kate said. "Nobody cared about what was happening and always told me I was lying."

As a result of the frequent sexual abuse, Kate began wetting the bed she shared with her siblings. As discipline, her mother would stretch her out on the kitchen table with help from her older siblings.

"My older brother, Billy, and older sister, Janice, stripped me naked and would pin me down on the table," she said of her mom's cruelty. "Then, my mom would thread a needle as she stood between my legs to tell me she was sewing up my genitals, and [she] stuck me with the needle until I cried myself unconscious."

Not only was her home life traumatic, but at her all-black school, Kate often would get beat up as one of the few white kids in her classroom. Since she changed schools so frequently, Kate had difficulty because she was often the "new kid" in class.

"I knew early on from the way I was raised that I would never raise my own child in that way," Kate vowed. "When my son was born, I loved him so much and was over-protective of him. Now he's 35 and the hardest thing I ever had to do was to let him go when he turned 18."

In an effort to escape more trauma when Rocky threatened to kidnap 17-year-old Kate and take her to Florida to marry him, Kate ran off with a "nice" man that she had recently met at the diner. He claimed he wanted to marry her as a platonic business deal. That way, the police would not bring her back home and he could help her escape her toxic family, he told her.

"So, he took me across the state line to Jackson, Tennessee, and we got married as agreed. Only, I didn't realize that he was a pedophile who had been grooming me," she said. "He raped and beat me beyond recognition, pulled out wads of my hair, and stomped on my stomach and fingers."

After several months, Kate was able to escape her husband's tight grip to a domestic violence shelter. She got a divorce through the help of Legal Aid and moved to Arizona with a fresh batch of emotional scars.

In recent years, Kate started sharing her life story on stage around the Los Angeles area. She found a way to turn trauma into triumph, which she coined as a "Tramedy," a hybrid of a comedic performance and the real trauma that she lived through. She said her performances have tremendously helped with her healing process.

"Later in life, I realized that our stories are the only thing that we own," Kate said. "Sharing my story gives the situation more meaning to help others."

Kate is currently working on her memoir, *How I Busted Out of My Genes and Changed My Life Story Forever.* She says her therapist marvels over how crystal clear her memories are from her dreadful childhood. She admits she is still discovering unhealthy behaviors in her life that have resulted from the emotional and physical childhood scars, and she welcomes their healing.

"I'm so glad I didn't kill myself because the #MeToo Movement has liberated me," she said. "And while it wasn't predictable, today I have joy."

Kate's mother died at age 79, on Kate's birthday. Kate says she does not stay in contact with her unstable siblings. Instead, she considers her network of close friends as her family.

"My husband, my two dogs, my son and my friends, are my true family," she explained. "Years later, with the help of a book called *Toxic Parents,* I wrote 11 confrontation letters to my family members — not for them, but for me — that helped to free me from the past. It really helped to transform my worldview and to begin to learn about malignant narcissism, being scapegoated, and family mobbing."

Kate finally discovered there was never anything wrong with her, the problem was always her toxic family.

"Looking inside myself, I found a good person, a lovable person," she said. "Not the ugly, stupid, good for nothing they told me I was."

Her Advice: "I want survivors to know that you are not a victim when you realize that you have options, and you can be in control of your own destiny, regardless of what anyone tells you or tries to make you believe."

***

Lasonya

"This is not fiction or entertainment, this is my actual life story," began Lasonya Love. "I lived this. It wasn't easy but I did."

Between the ages of 5 and 12, she was sexually abused by her step-grandfather, her cousin, her uncle's friend and even her brother. She remembers that the high-traffic environment in her Grandma Rose's Detroit house left her vulnerable to many potential predators.

"My mom was a young mother with a substance abuse problem, and when I was just three months old, my sister and I were sent to live with my grandma," she said. "I always felt like my mom couldn't stand me and that she wished she had aborted me."

These nagging negative feelings created emotional problems throughout Lasonya's life. And it caused her to feel like the black sheep of the family.

"Early on, Grandma Rose's husband John took a special interest in me and began molesting me at age 5," she explained. "I would cry and beg for my grandma not to leave me at home with him but she still would."

Lasonya never knew who her biological father was, and some family members told her that John was actually *her* father. But, Lasonya didn't know what to make of the conflicting stories so the truth remains a mystery in her family.

"When I tried to tell my grandma about the molestation, she was dismissive of my story," Lasonya said. "I even think my sister witnessed our grandfather trying to pull my pajamas down one day. But I think she tried blocked it out of her mind in denial."

Around the same time, her 16-year-old cousin Edward, also began molesting Lasonya even in the presence of other kids in their family.

"Soon, Edward started making my brother, Mario, do stuff to me as well," she admitted. "I think these things easily went on in secret because there was always a lot of drinking going on with the adults. My uncle had a lot of friends that would come over to get drunk and shoot pool."

As if Lasonya hadn't suffered enough trauma, she began to endure more abuse from a fourth predator a few years later. Sixteen-year-old Frank, her uncle's childhood friend, who frequently came over and focused much of his attention on Lasonya.

"He took me into my grandma's bathroom and began to molest me on the bathroom floor," Lasonya said. "But his sister spotted us so the abuse didn't last too long that day. His sister later told me that she suspected Frank was abusing me."

Lasonya's premature sexual experiences led to her first pregnancy by age 16 and her second just two years later at age 18.

"I was a young mother and I had taken on a lot of guilt about all of the abuse I dealt with," she explained. "I later understood that it was not my fault, but only after attempting to commit suicide twice."

Lasonya says she in her early twenties, she struggled emotionally and financially as a single mom. She suffered "agonizing pain" when she would think about her difficult childhood and her lack of family support.

"The problem was that I didn't know how to love myself," she said, thinking back to her adolescence. "In order to save myself, I had to first get rid of the guilt I had carried with me through the years."

Lasonya realized Grandma Rose's denial of her abuse was a pain point for her. Years later, when her ailing grandmother was on her deathbed, Lasonya yearned to ask her why she never believed the abuse claims.

"But I couldn't get up the courage to ask her about it. I thought it would have been selfish of me to ask and have *that* be one of her final memories of me," Lasonya remembered.

In 2002, later in her life, she was dating an unstable man who shot her two times in the chest after a surprising and angry tirade. God saw it fit that Lasonya not only survive four childhood abusers, but also devastating domestic violence as an adult. Lasonya faced a long road to physical and emotional recovery after the shooting attack.

"Later in life, I tried to face my abusers, although Edward denied ever molesting me," she said. "And my brother wrote me a 20-page apology letter when he was in prison, which I did forgive him."

Lasonya, who is now an active grandparent, forgave Grandpa John although he died years ago. She also forgave Edward after reconnecting at a family reunion in Memphis years later.

"I never truly understood the extent of what I had gone through until much later as an adult," said Lasonya, who is in the early stage of writing her only life story. "But, I thank God for keeping me through it all."

Lasonya's trials have spurred her to work with young women at her church and in her community through various organizations.

"We have a lot of people out here suffering in silence. After my abuse, I wanted to really wanted to see people get healed," said the married 46-year-old. "I try to be an example of someone who spiritually and mentally cleansed."

Her Advice: "You must believe through faith that ALL things are possible, no matter the time or space!"

***

Karla

Karla Robertson survived a family history of incest. She even recalls living next door to a family where the father impregnated his own daughter. Thus, sexual abuse was a difficult and very real part of her childhood environment.

Karla was sexually abused by her grandfather Ernest and her 20-year-old Uncle Bobby between the ages of 7 and 10. Karla was raised in Detroit by her single mother and remembers when her grandfather moved in and became her new babysitter.

"My grandfather would play with my chest while my mom worked nights," she recalled of the 50-something-year-old man. "I probably didn't know how to directly tell her, but when I did approach my mom, she said, 'Just do what he says because I need him to babysit you and your sister.'"

Karla says her uncle and grandfather, who were both alcoholics, attempted to molest her sister, too. But she recalled that most of the inappropriate touching was largely focused on her.

"Looking back, this was a very confusing part of my childhood because they never made me feel like they were hurting me," she explained. "I trusted them because of who they were to me. Plus, I was always taught to respect your elders."

Karla's grandfather died when she was 13, and his death brought up feelings of guilt from her mother. Her mom, who forgot about Karla's first attempt to tell her years before, even blamed her teenage daughter for her own abuse, saying, "You should have told me sooner."

"My grandfather and uncle kept me quiet with guilt, saying stuff like, 'Your mom is going to kill me if she ever finds out about this,'" she said. "I was angry about all of that for a long time and it affected me in a variety of ways."

The 50-year-old mother and grandmother says the biggest repercussion was that she didn't trust ANY men for a long time.

"I was in my twenties before I even felt comfortable using sexual language," she admits. "Because of my experiences, I viewed all men as nasty in my early years."

In 2014, Karla was diagnosed with Stage 4 lung cancer after 25 years as a smoker. However, after an aggressive three months of treatment, doctors said her cancer had miraculously disappeared.

"I told my doctors that I didn't want to be a victim. I would say, 'No, I'm not going to die,'" said Karla. She refused to let both cancer and sexual abuse get the best of her.

"Today, I truly thank God for my healing, and I have a lot of women come to me for advice about their cancer."

Her Advice: "Pray about who you leave your children with. Don't make important decisions like that out of need."

***

Renee

Renee Newton regrets not telling her family about the way her step-grandfather molested her as a child. If she had broken her silence sooner, Renee believes she may have saved other family members from facing abuse.

As a preteen, Renee dealt with unwanted touching by her step-grandfather, William, whenever she would visit her grandparents' house. This went on throughout her adolescent years.

"When I would stay overnight, I had to sleep in the bed in between my grandparents," she explained. "As my grandmother slept, William would take that opportunity to feel all over me. This went on for a duration of about five years."

Renee wondered whether William was also abusing her female cousins, but she remained silent about the molestation because he always told her not to tell her mother and grandmother.

"Grandma didn't know anything was going on," she recalled. "William even offered me money to keep me quiet."

"Years later, William came back up in a conversation with family and we discovered that he was doing the same thing to my cousins," she lamented. "I never addressed it with Grandma, in order to spare her feelings. I also thought that Grandma might kill me so I got too scared to bring it up later on."

As a married mother of two young daughters, Renee says that every mom needs to be on alert for the "sickies" out there. She believes parents really can't trust many people around your kids these days.

"Even now, parents need to be even more careful than when I was coming up about who their children are around," she said. "She recalls how her old babysitter's husband was forcing their daughters to give him oral sex. And he also forced his step-daughter into having sex with him."

Renee is an avid supporter of the #MeToo Movement, but questions why such support for female survivors took so long to organize.

"I feel like families just don't say anything and they care more about reputation than the safety of children," she said. "I feel like now, finally, people are listening more than before!"

Her Advice: "Sharing your stories is powerful. If you hold your story in, then you can't help anybody. If I would have told my story sooner, perhaps my step-grandfather could have sought help."

***

Barb

With much clarity, Barb remembers how her creepy grandfather abused her and her siblings individually when they were growing up. She also says, "There's no doubt in my mind that my sister's nervous breakdown was attributed to the child abuse Grandpa Arthur caused."

Growing up in New York as part of a big family meant that Barb and her siblings religiously visited her grandparents' house every week for Sunday dinner.

"Unfortunately, this always meant we had to go back into my grandfather's room to put our coats on the bed," Barb recalled. "I distinctly remember trying to bolt in and out, yet he would always corner us on the way out of the room."

Barb despised the way their mother would dress the girls for their frequent visits to see their grandparents. She recalls being about eight years old at the time.

"We all *had* to wear dresses!" She explained, which gave her perverted grandfather easy access to their underwear. "My mom had a very traditional view. And that wouldn't have been a problem if he wasn't always grabbing us and tickling us inappropriately."

Even now, she is always so relieved to see mothers dress their daughters in stretch pants beneath their skirts and dresses. She views it as a layer of protection.

"One time," Barb said in her East Coast accent, "I distinctly remember that for once my grandmother had observed my grandpa's bad behavior and she yelled at him, saying, 'Arthur! You leave those babies alone right now. We were so young and we didn't have the tools to process everything. Plus, he would say: 'Don't bother telling anyone, they don't want to know.'"

The child abuse had a damaging and lasting effect on Barb and her siblings -- which showed back up when Grandpa Arthur died at age 90.

"I was living in Florida and I was still afraid to go back to New York with my infant son," she recalled. "So, I was relieved when my mom said, 'Don't worry about coming back for the funeral.'"

Barb contends that her mom never properly dealt with the concept of her father being a molester the way she should have.

"One of my sisters did try to tell Mom later on, but Mom's response was, 'I can't handle that,'" Barb said. "Even back then, I think there was no way my mom and Grandma didn't know something was going on."

Years later, the molestation she endured made Barb hypersensitive when it came to her son being with child care providers. Her ex-husband was also uncomfortable with having a lot of different babysitters in their home.

"I was in denial for so many years about this," said Barb, now 59. "The abuse made me a very unaffectionate kid and I really missed some fun aspects of my childhood. I feel robbed in many ways!"

Barb now lives in West Palm Beach, Florida, and works as a bookkeeper. She said that her child abuse and the #MeToo Movement has inspired her to get involved with a local organization that helps prevent child abuse.

Her Advice: "I want people to wake up a bit more. People need to open their eyes to see what's really going on around them."

The Last Word

Many adult survivors have lived through unthinkable incidents and pain. Survivors of child abuse often face deep and difficult wounds, as well as a life-long journey of healing. Though we may not realize it, survivors are people we interact with every day. They are your siblings, neighbors, co-workers, or your children's teachers.

After experiencing such trauma, some abused children have a difficult time understanding who they are, particularly in instances when they're hurt by people who should love them. Experts say adult survivors of child abuse often go through three stages: remembering, mourning, and healing. These stages often include many baby steps along the way.

From a parental perspective, it's not always easy to identify or cope with a child's sexual abuse. It can be even more daunting when you suspect someone close to you. Find a local sexual assault service provider if you are in need of advice. But the most important and practical step is removing your child from potentially unsafe situations.

Hallie Sheffey has counseled scores of abuse survivors in West Michigan over the years. "In my professional experience, I have found that some black parents tend not to believe their children when it comes to abuse," she says. "Parents often say, 'So-and-so is lying or being over-dramatic,' when they should *always* assume that young people are telling the truth about abuse."

Sheffey explains that many kids tend to tell their story in pieces so it's important to let them share it their own way.

"As a parent, believe your child, support them, and try your best to keep your kids safe," she said. "And don't be afraid to talk to your family members if you need to. I know it's not easy sometimes but it has to be done."

Some survivors interviewed sought validation by sharing the abuse with parents or close adults, but they were usually not believed. This experience can be devastating for children and cause trust issues.

What's more, if your family members failed to protect you, or worse, were the perpetrators, then it can cause deep-seated self-doubt. As a defense mechanism, some parents of abused kids avoid responsibility or guilt by blaming children and ignoring the truth of abuse once they become aware of it. But in a healthy environment, the parents are the ones who are supposed to nurture kids, make kids feel valued, and give them a sense of worthiness.

As a society, we specifically have to teach young women not to doubt or second-guess themselves when it comes to abusive situations.

Signs to Look for in Children

The major factor in protecting your child from abuse is identifying warning signs. It's critical to TRUST your INSTINCT if there is something you've observed that you're unsure about or a sense of discomfort. Be vigilant about the adults who spend time with your children. Be on alert, for instance, if adults appear to be too friendly with your children or are excessively interested in them, make sexual comments, or buy them gifts.

Here are red flags that indicate your child may be experiencing abuse:

- Frequent medical attention

- Sexually transmitted diseases

- Genital bruising or bleeding

- Inappropriate sexual behavior

- Fear of being left alone with people

- Fear of undressing

- Knowledge about sexual topics

- Nightmares

When it comes to alleged child abuse, you are never alone. If you suspect abuse, reach out to an organization trained to help you. Please reference the list of resource organizations in the last chapter.

CHAPTER THREE

Acquaintance Rape

"Half my life, I have been zipping up my smile hoping you don't think I want to unzip your jeans."
-Ashley Judd

What is the typical profile of a sexual predator? Some experts say there is no actual profile because the perpetrator can be a man or woman, stranger or friend of victims. "Date rape," or acquaintance rape, is defined as a rape that takes place between two people who know each other.

Acquaintance rape is a growing problem on college campuses around the country, largely because of the roles that drinking, recreational drugs, and the party culture play. The graph below indicates that seven out of 10 rape victims previously knew their attacker.

It can be a daunting task to protect yourself from these attacks because there is often established trust that causes survivors to let their guard down.

Acquaintance rape is grossly under-reported because some survivors question the gravity of the assault since their perpetrator has a familiar or even friendly face.

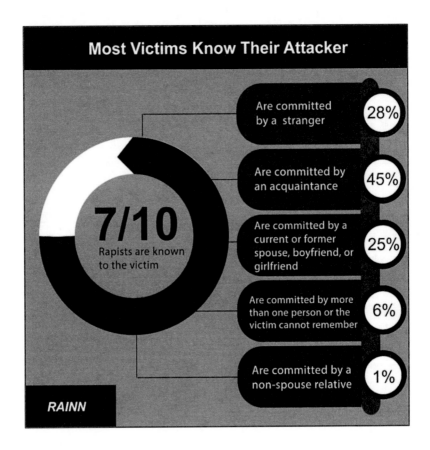

Most Victims Know Their Attacker

7/10
Rapists are known
to the victim

Are committed by a stranger — 28%

Are committed by an acquaintance — 45%

Are committed by a current or former spouse, boyfriend, or girlfriend — 25%

Are committed by more than one person or the victim cannot remember — 6%

Are committed by a non-spouse relative — 1%

RAINN

Survivors should NOT disregard experiences, EVEN IF:

- You knew the perpetrator prior to the incident

- The encounter started out consensual

- You never said "No"

- One or both of you were under the influence of drugs or alcohol

- You felt guilty afterward

- You didn't file a police report

- The incident happened many years ago

- You've never labeled the incident sexual violence

- You have uncertainty about the incident

If you've been raped, it is important to share the incident with a hotline, crisis center or therapist in your community. If fear or judgment is holding you back from reporting your experience, it's important to remember that other potential victims also benefit from you sharing details of your sexual assault.

***

Constance

Constance Johnston was gang-raped in a dark room on her first day at Alabama State University, over a decade ago. She has been raped four times throughout her lifetime, by boyfriends or men familiar to her. This, along with the fact that the first rape occurred at the ripe age of 11, has attributed to a long, emotional road for her. After multiple failed suicide attempts, Constance considers it a blessing that she is still standing to resiliently tell her story.

When Constance was 11 and growing up in Montgomery, Alabama, she was gaining local notoriety for her "Say No to Drugs" song and her "Black History" song. When a schoolmate suggested that she meet a man who could help her make it, she thought it was a good idea.

"Looking back, it's pretty amazing that this 20-something-year-old man was hanging around my elementary school in plain sight of teachers," Constance said. "He was a master manipulator and he would tell me, 'Your family doesn't love you, but I love you!'"

Constance says her innocence led her to believe everything he said. And one day, he came up to the school and the two of them walked to his house nearby. He raped Constance and then walked her back to the school.

"I was devastated, and my mother was too," she began. "When she filed a police report, the officer said that they would do all that they could, but I don't even know if they really did."

Constance and her mother experienced a backlash in their community. Some people suggested that the rape was her mom's fault, while others pointed a finger at Constance by saying she "was a fast girl."

"I'll never forget," said Constance, "one woman told me, 'I don't care if you were 9, 10 or 11 and naked running down the street. A man should never touch a child.'" She explained how "even though this was told to me years later, it still helped to lift a heavy weight off of me."

At 17, Constance was living with her sister in North Carolina and dating a significantly older man whom she had recently met. Her new boyfriend had a good job and two teenage daughters. He invited her to his house for the first time as a "double date." But upon arrival, things were not what they seemed.

"By the time I got to his house, my boyfriend's cousin was arguing with a crying woman, saying: 'I said that you always get your money first,'" Constance recalled. "With his daughters upstairs, he suddenly told me to come out to the garage with him, where he raped me."

Constance was shocked at the way her boyfriend completely changed from this sweet man into a sexually-charged monster. And when she asked him to take her home, he refused to help her.

"I thought you said you loved me?" Constance yelled. "Why would you treat me this way?"

He then told her that he never loved her. He took her money and raped her a second time. Since she couldn't afford a cab, Constance left his house on foot, hoping to find a ride back to her sister's house. She was relieved after a few minutes when a passer-by picked her up as she walked through the neighborhood.

"I was really upset and I began telling the guy what had just happened to me," Constance said. "I told him where I needed to be dropped off, but then he started to drive in a different direction. Then, he locked the doors as he started touching himself!"

Constance couldn't take any more trauma and started to strike the man as hard as she could. Then she unlocked his door and ran away as fast as her heels would carry her. By the time she did make it home, Constance locked herself away to cry in her bedroom and decided to swallow four bottles of pills. Her suicide attempt was foiled when her sister broke into her room and discovered that Constance had passed out. The ambulance took her to a nearby hospital for a few days to recover.

Two years later was Constance's first day as a freshman at Alabama State University. She spent most of the day on campus getting settled in her dorm room and the rest of it socializing as most new students do. She met a particular student, a senior, who had been hanging around her dorm.

"'You new here?' he asked me," she recalled. "'Yes,' I told him. Then he asked, 'Do you want to hang out and go for a ride?'"

Constance responded with a "Yes," and off they went in his car. She attributed her willingness to go with him to her naivety and the fact that he was a senior showing interest in her.

"I expected that he would drive me around when he drove to a nearby apartment building," Constance said. "He asked me to come in but I told him I wasn't sure if I should. Then he reassured me that we'd only be there for a minute, so I went."

Constance recalls that the apartment was dark because all of the blinds were closed and the lights were off. Suddenly, two other men ran out of the bathroom toward her and proceeded to strip off Constance's clothes and rape her.

"I was so scared, but one guy had my mouth covered so I couldn't scream," she recalled. "I kept begging them to take me home but they just kept assaulting me."

The 19-year-old was visibly upset but the group of college friends didn't seem to care. And when he was ready, the senior took her back to campus.

"Welcome to Alabama State," he chuckled when he dropped her back off at her dormitory. "The very next day, I marched straight into a female counselor's office on campus and she responded with no empathy, and a question: 'Are you interested in getting these boys in trouble?'"

That painful response spurred Constance to withdraw at the registrar's office immediately after leaving the counselor. Then she called her mother to tell her that she would be coming home. But a few days later, before leaving, she received a phone call from the senior.

"He said he was very sorry about what had happened and that he wanted to make it up to me," Constance explained. "He kept asking me so I agreed to meet him again."

This time, the senior took her to a house and when Constance resisted coming inside, the big dude literally carried her into the dark house. She recalls that there were a lot of students standing around the room.

"Again, he proceeds to rape me while some of the other guys joined in or pinned me down," Constance tearfully recalled. "I can't even tell you how many men raped me because it seemed like a lot."

This time, on their way back to her dorm, Constance threatened to tell the police but the senior seemed cocky and unscathed by her threats. She never did file a police report on either incident, but that is commonplace when it comes to sexual violence among college students. According to a recent University of Iowa study, only about 7% of college rapes are reported to authorities.

"I didn't care about my body anymore," Constance said of the low self-esteem that she struggled with after experiencing so much sexual violence. "I really wanted to be loved and I suffered horribly after experiencing so much trauma."

At times, Constance admits that her life reads much like a dramatic biography -- including two occasions when she was committed to a mental institution.

"I've been hospitalized numerous times when I experienced mental breakdowns," she explained. "When my daughter was just six months old, my family took her away to care for her a while because they felt that I was unstable."

Now, Constance's life with her daughter is much happier and her self-esteem has greatly improved.

"Before the #MeToo Movement, I never felt free enough to tell my whole story," said Constance, who has published three books and writes poetry. "But after I started hearing about all of the celebrity stories, I felt like now I am a small fish swimming in a very big pond!"

By the grace of God, the 33-year-old single mother has survived rape, a house fire, a flipped-car accident, and suicide attempts. With pride, she says she is currently working toward her doctorate degree.

"I did return to Alabama State to finally earn my degree," said Constance with joy. "I went on to become president of the Honor Society, and I've also won various poetry contests."

Constance acknowledges still having a long way to go with the healing process. But she has found great solace in a healing and restoration program at her church.

"By the time I'm 40, I'll be Dr. Constance Johnston," she said with pride. "Soon I will be leading a bible study at my church for abuse survivors."

Her Advice: "I want to tell younger people not to rush into adulthood. You'll get there soon enough."

***

Erica

Sometimes neighbors aren't always neighborly. Erica Carrington learned the hard way that sometimes the people in close proximity can pose a great danger to you.

The summer that Erica turned 17, her parents lived next door to a group of college friends. One of the college students would get frequent visits from his older brother, who was in his early 30s.

"I remember how they would have these ranging block parties most weekends, all summer long," Erica recalled, "The adults and us teens would get really drunk. The older brother was grooming me by sneaking alcohol to me at the parties."

Their trusting friendship grew as the brother began periodically offering Erica rides home from work. Then he offered to help Erica secretly get a cell phone of her own.

"When my parents wouldn't allow me to attend a concert without an adult present, he offered to buy my ticket and serve as my adult chaperone," she explained. "After the concert, he walked me up to my front door but wouldn't let me go inside. Instead, he insisted that I go with him into the backyard. Then, he trapped me and he proceeded to rape me on top of the air conditioning unit."

Erica recalled the pain she felt because the unit was still running. She felt the unit burning her skin while the assault was happening. She remembered wearing a sundress that her mother hated because it was on the shorter side.

"I vividly remembered the way the unit's metal slats dug into my ass and thighs," she said. "It was really sore and left red and purple indentations on my body."

Like many survivors, Erica didn't completely realize that she had been raped afterward because "I was drunk and he was nice to me."

"I didn't call it rape and I didn't tell my parents until I was in my late 20s," she said. "The news came out at a really tough emotional time when I was going through a divorce and an unplanned pregnancy."

The sexual violence she experienced as a teenager later contributed to her struggle with severe anxiety and depression.

"What's worse is, my parents said they didn't believe me because they thought I was just seeking extra attention," Erica said reluctantly.

***

Tana

At 22, Tana Session was raped at gunpoint by an angry ex-boyfriend. A decade earlier, she was raped at age 13 by a teenage family friend.

In the early 1980s, you could find 13-year-old Tana on her bedroom floor still playing with her black Barbie dolls. She lived in a small town in South Carolina and her mother was dating a man who would often bring his high-school-aged nephew, Billy, over with him.

"Although I had a cousin who molested me at age 7, I wasn't remotely interested in sex," Tana said of the time her mom and her mom's boyfriend left her alone in their apartment with Billy. "He called me into the room to show me something on TV and had pulled his penis out."

Tana pleaded with him, saying she was still a virgin, but he responded by saying: "That's why you need to find out what this feels like."

Billy forcefully threw Tana onto her mother's bed and proceeded to pull off her pants.

"Then he began jamming himself inside of me," Tana recalled. "And while he's raping me, Billy began saying, 'Don't bother telling anyone about this because no one is going to believe you.'"

Tana started bawling uncontrollably because Billy told her that everyone at school would think she was a ho and think she was a liar.

"At that moment, I realized that blood was streaming down my leg," Tana said of the sexual trauma. "He told me to pull myself together, while at the same time he reminded me how wealthy his family was and that no one would believe my story because we were poor."

Tana said that at the time, her family was living on welfare and to some extent she believed the lies he told her.

"I only told my good friend at school and my mom had no clue," she said. "After that, I would always make up excuses about why I didn't want to be around Billy anymore. My mom seemed to believe me."

But by the time Tana was 22, she was raped again, only this time by her ex-boyfriend whom she had dated for about a year. Unbeknownst to Tana, her ex-boyfriend had closely trailed behind someone through the security door of her Brooklyn apartment building and hid near her door until she came home from work.

"The second I slipped my key in the lock, I felt a gun to my back," Tana recalled. "He started choking me while telling me that he still loved me. He then placed his gun on my nightstand and told me that he didn't really want to hurt me."

But he had a firm chokehold on Tana and she quickly began to lose consciousness. She blacked out and her eyes began to roll into the back of her head. He eventually let go of her neck and Tana began gasping for air. Her ex-boyfriend continued to rape her until he forced her to take a shower.

"I think he knew that I was going to call the police so he wanted me to erase the evidence," Tana explained. "But he failed to realize that I avoided washing my vagina before he left."

The next day, a dazed Tana filed a police report and the police immediately wanted to set up a sting operation to arrest him. A few days later, an armed team of police officers silently followed Tana into her ex-boyfriend's house where he was arrested. This outcome is significant because of all the 20 stories in this book, Tana's story is the only one that resulted in a conviction and prison time.

"A sample of his semen was found during my medical review," Tana said. "I don't even know how long he went to Riker's Island, but they arrested him on assault and a gun charge because his gun was not registered."

Tana, who is now married to hip-hop pioneer Dana Dane, believes she had an out-of-body experience when her ex-boyfriend choked her. At the time, she assumed that it was going to be the way she died.

"I knew that if I could just lie there and deal with it, I could make it through," Tana explained. "These traumas I endured showed up for me later in life in a variety of ways. At one point, sex wasn't as joyful as it should have been."

Tana, who is an internationally known speaker and transformation coach, uses all of her experiences to boldly elevate the lives of other women. After therapy and coaching support, Tana now views her back story as the "secret sauce" that helps her to motivate other women. Tana's motto is: "Focus on your goals, Propel to the next level of success and activate your true potential."

Her Advice: "Women need to stop judging other women and stop blaming women victims. I'm glad that now women aren't afraid to tell their stories."

***

Debra

Dr. Debra Guckenheimer was raped by her "friend" whom she met during an organized trip to Israel for American Jewish young adults. About a year after the trip, Debra returned to Israel to live and study at the Hebrew University of Jerusalem and the friend offered for her to stay at his family's home to get acclimated before her program started. Her first night back in Israel, he raped her while she was sleeping.

"After he raped me, he tried to convince me that nothing bad had happened," she said. "He even stalked me for a while because I naturally didn't want to be friends anymore."

But when Debra went to the Israeli police to report the assault, the officer accused the 21-year-old American of lying. She chose to believe the perpetrator, who was serving in Israel's military.

"Staff on programs like the ones I attended don't get training about handling sexual violence," Debra explained. "I didn't know where to turn for help. I eventually found a rape crisis center on my own after a year."

Debra, who is now 42, explained that being in a new country without support led her to go into denial about what had happened to her.

"I do wish that I would have recognized earlier how much being raped would impact me," she admitted. "I think there often is a resistance to accepting how much trauma you've actually been through."

Despite the hardship, Debra lived in Israel for 3½ years before returning home. She thinks the isolation of being in a new country and her delay in getting good treatment contributed to the impact the rape had on her.

"Sometimes I just couldn't believe that I was raped," she admitted. "I was just stubborn. I didn't want my perpetrator to have power over me and chase me out of the country."

While rape impacts every community, it is important to interrogate aspects of culture which support sexual violence. For instance, Debra says she often sees Jewish parents give their daughters different rules and earlier curfews to follow than their sons. These practices can create a lot of blame and shame for young women in instances where sexual violence does occur.

"Sexual violence is almost never talked about in the Jewish community," said Debra. "There's an idea that Jewish women and girls are safer around Jewish men and boys, but research shows that sexual violence occurs at rates similar in the Jewish community to any other community."

Debra would like to see every community, including her own, start to address sexual violence head on to better support survivors and to prevent future sexual assaults.

"All Jewish organizations should talk about sexual assault, not just those organizing trips to Israel," Debra stated. "I think that in the future, similar to the Catholic Church, we'll see a lot more scandals uncovered. There have already been a couple but they just haven't been widely publicized."

Debra has also seen cases of sexual abuse in the Jewish community where, after being charged with sexual abuse, a perpetrator changes their name and quickly moves to start the cycle of abuse over again.

"Many Jewish organizations don't even require background checks," she explained. "Some don't even have policies in place around sexual abuse offenses of clergy, staff, and leaders."

Debra, who is a sociologist and an expert in diversity and inclusion, has a decade of experience with organizations serving survivors of sexual violence and doing prevention work. She hopes that her story inspires support for survivors and efforts to prevent future sexual assaults. She lives in California with her spouse, child, and two dogs.

Her Advice: "It's healthier to acknowledge being sexually assaulted. I always tell survivors that the only way to heal is to deal with it head on."

The Last Word

It's important for a survivor to seek medical attention after a sexual assault. In addition to getting a thorough examination, often DNA samples and physical evidence can be obtained and preserved for legal purposes.

U.S. statistics show that more than half of sexual assaults made by familiar predators are never reported to authorities. Moreover, a sexual crime reported within 24 hours has a much greater chance of providing sufficient evidence for a conviction. But beyond 72 hours after an assault, the survivor is at higher risk of losing DNA evidence. Reporting the crime within 24 hours helps to increase the chance of investigation, prosecution and conviction.

Rape survivors often get bogged down by shame, blame themselves, or feel like "damaged goods" after an assault. They may experience physical side effects like sleeping problems and emotional distress. In addition, sexual assault survivors are:

- More likely to suffer from depression

- More likely to suffer from Post-Traumatic Stress Syndrome

- More likely to abuse alcohol or drugs

- More likely to attempt suicide

According to the Rape Crisis Network's 2015 statistic, about 85% of sexual assaults are attributed to a known perpetrator. Knowing the perpetrator greatly contributes to the under-reporting of attempted or completed sexual assaults. Therefore, rape victims must protect themselves against "friends," ex-lovers, neighbors, classmates, and the like.

This was true of Constance, Erica, Tana and Debra. In my interview with retired therapist Hallie Sheffey, she recalled a number of stories where clients were sexually assaulted by family members.

"I remember working with a college student whose uncle would come to campus and rape her," Sheffey, referring to a young woman who was raised by her sexual predator. "Her parents were drug addicts and her uncle made her feel indebted. So, she would just let her uncle have his way with her."

The fact that her uncle was paying for her college education was the bind that he held over her, and it deterred her from reporting him to authorities.

"For some rape victims, they feel like they were murdered," Sheffey said. "One client said she couldn't sleep well after her assault because she didn't know whether her intruders would come back to attack again."

Sheffey described the violation some rape survivors feel to being naked in front of the entire world.

"I tell survivors not to let their perpetrator take their dignity from them," she explained firmly. "I remind them not to live in fear because on some level that allows them to win."

Protecting Yourself

It's important to use a high level of awareness, self-discipline and common sense when it comes to protecting yourself against acquaintance rape. Since statistics show that half of all rapes are premeditated, it's important to avoid predicaments where you are alone with someone you don't know well.

"I don't want people to think any particular precaution will necessarily keep you 100% safe," said Hallie Sheffey, who worked as a therapist for 45 years in Michigan. "But, for example, college students can monitor their alcohol consumption, avoid leaving their drink unattended, and remember to designate a point person to drive if they drink too much."

Staying sober on first dates or at parties can be an important safeguard when it comes to the role of alcohol and drugs in sexual assault. Above all, TRUST yourself! Many survivors report having "a bad feeling" before a sexual assault occurred. Following your better judgment could mean the difference between a life or death situation.

"In this social media age, people give out too much personal information," said Sheffey. "There are things we can do to help us stay safe. One thing I do is communicate my schedule or travel info to at least one other person when I'm alone."

Perpetrators never expect their victims to share information about their whereabouts with family or friends, she said. Sheffey warns women to do whatever they can to prevent assault.

CHAPTER FOUR

Religious Ties

"I think the issue of clergy sexual abuse sparked people to look at their faith in a different way."
- Rev. William P. Leahy

What would Jesus say about the widespread abuse that women, men, and children face today? As a Christian, I would guess Jesus would say, "No More," and would stand with the oppressed and assaulted victims. Unfortunately, our society can point to recent scandals of sexual abuse involving high-profile bishops, clergy and church leaders. This includes Bishop Eddie Long, Pastor Bob Coy, and former Sovereign Grace Ministry president C.J. Mahaney.

Across many denominations and faiths, the collective church has had a checkered history regarding abuse. We know that in some incidents, church leaders tried to cover up abuse instead of dealing with it honestly in the public.

Nearly 20 years ago, I remember when the news broke of my own 40-something pastor's affair and sexual assault case with a fellow teenage church member. The inappropriate and shocking affair would go on for several years. The late Rev. Robert Eckert was my married pastor who was well-respected around West Michigan in the late 1990s. However, after the teen's family brought a lawsuit and damning headlines broke in the media, the fallen pastor would be best remembered as a sexual predator. He eventually received a prison sentence of up to 15 years and dragged my church's good name into the mud. But most importantly, he took advantage of a young and innocent church member by abusing his position as a religious leader.

In the 1990s, child sexual abuse gained international attention for cases in the U.S., Canada, Ireland, and beyond. In many cases, known pedophiles were just slapped on the wrist and transferred from diocese to diocese. By the late 2000s, CBS News reported that the central governing body of the Catholic Church had received more than 3,000 sex abuse allegation cases.

Sadly, there have been many incidents where believers (and non-believers) have turned to the church and church leaders for support, only to be met with disbelief or completely ignored. In numerous instances, the collective church has often sided with the perpetrators and those in power instead of the powerless and the oppressed.

Sexual abuse certainly tarnishes the faith of many followers and dims the bright light that the broader faith community provides. True, church leaders are human like everybody else; however, when they are elevated to god-like heights, that's where the problem begins.

***

Froswa

Dr. Froswa Booker-Drew was an avid church-goer, but after a disturbing incident with the pastor of her prominent Church of God in Christ church, she stopped going for years. At the time, she was unaware that the pastor had a secret sexual fetish and was a known sexual predator toward women in his congregation.

Froswa, who at the time was a 20-year-old college student at the University of Texas at Arlington, had scheduled a counseling appointment with the pastor one afternoon at the church in the Dallas-Fort Worth metroplex.

"Instead of receiving spiritual guidance, the pastor abruptly told me, 'You are a bad girl and you need a spanking," explained Froswa. "The pastor proceeded to chase me around his office, trying to catch me."

Froswa was shocked and scared, even though the pair weren't alone. The pastor's secretary was sitting nearby. Frowsa said, "[When it comes to men who are sexual predators] There always seems to be a woman nearby to help create an illusion of safety."

Froswa wondered if the pastor's inappropriate behavior was attributed to the fact that she wore her particular red skirt and blouse. She also felt the fact that her parents lived several hours away could have played a part. "I think Pastor thought that I would be an easy target because I was an out of state student. No, this wasn't a physical violation, but it most certainly was a spiritual one."

Froswa came straight home and told her boyfriend (who is now her husband) about the pastor's shocking behavior. Her boyfriend wanted to hurt him, and the couple was quite disappointed because they both looked up to the 30-something pastor as a trusted spiritual leader.

Froswa believes it is problematic that many churches don't have policies in place or protocol to follow in situations like these.

"I remember that I kept showering because I really felt dirty after that ordeal," she said. "I didn't have a bad reputation, but through his words, he really made me feel nasty."

She only told a handful of people close to her about the incident, and some encouraged her to take action. Initially, Froswa didn't think that escalating the matter would help because the experience had been emotionally draining. It took a while to recover.

"I started wearing bigger clothing and questioned myself in a lot of ways," she explained. "And I think that harassment situations can cause some women to gain weight, which can allow a person to hide as a form of protection."

Later, Froswa did make an appointment to speak to the bishop about the incident. She was stunned by his response after she described her encounter.

"The bishop said, 'Oh, he's doing that again? He's already had counseling, so we'll just be sure to get him some more counseling then.'"

The bishop had said this in a very nonchalant tone. There were no real repercussions to the pastor's harassment. And even though she was unsatisfied with his response and the outcome, Froswa eventually started attending church again.

"I never stopped having a relationship with God, but I stopped attending church altogether for years," she said. "If I could go back in time, I would tell myself, 'You did nothing wrong and you are going to get through this."

After the incident, Froswa learned of many other harassment complaints. "I wish he would have served time for all of the women he hurt over the years. As it turned out, the pastor had court cases against him for years. Looking back, I would have told more people about Pastor's behavior. Back then, there wasn't today's groundswell of women coming together to fight for women's causes," she said. "When it comes to the #MeToo Movement, I think we have a culture that is perverted and a culture that is unwilling to deal with creating boundaries."

Frowsa is now 47-year-old and works in the field of community affairs and development. She says she uses her harassment experience to help other women who feel a sense of brokenness.

Frowsa has been a writer since she was a kid. She is the author of *Rules of Engagement Making Connections Last,* and *Ready for a Revolution: 30 Days to Jolt Your Life.*

"I published a workbook for women that helps them find out who they are," she says. "Writing has been therapeutic."

Her Advice: "Look at the stories you are telling people about yourself. When you see yourself as a victim, you can draw people into your life who further victimize and use you. Also, use your voice. Many women internalize guilt and shame. Too many women have been silenced. Your story matters."

***

Alia

Last year, social justice activist Alia Salem and her business partner, formed an organization called Facing Abuse in Community Environments (FACE) after they learned of a clergy member in their community who was involved with a much younger female congregant. They were troubled by this news because just as a therapist has strict rules about relationships with their clients, the same code of conduct applies to clergy members.

"We got involved because this was a severe religious ethical violation," explained Alia, who is 38 and a graduate of the University of Texas at Arlington. "We soon realized that there was no community-based infrastructure to investigative this case, no community nonprofits that would touch this or support this woman with any lasting effect."

FACE provides a safe avenue of reporting abuse, investigation, education and resolution to address abuse claims. It is a ground-breaking organization which serves as an independent first line of support for victims in the Muslim community and beyond.

"When people go after religious leaders, they are often immediately looked at as troublemakers," she explained. "This is largely because the religious community puts its leaders on a pedestal and those leaders are often well loved."

Alia says this unrealistic view of religious leaders was also problematic with sexual abuse cases in the Catholic community when widespread abuse was uncovered in the 1990s. Catholic leaders are viewed as God's divinely chosen people, which means it's difficult for many followers to even think abuse is possible.

"It's hard for the community to believe claims of abuse because they are hearing the word [of God] flowing from their mouths like water," she said. "And in some cases, the institutional leadership isn't doing a good job of stopping abusers from going from mosque to mosque when accusations surface."

As Co-founder and President of FACE, Alia is fiercely passionate about seeking justice for those who can't fight these daunting battles alone. Her Texas-based 501(c)3 assists women who are experiencing abuse by religious leaders or institutions in their community.

Also, as a survivor of abuse herself, Alia has a unique perspective when it comes to helping other survivors. She endured abuse as a child as well as abuse by her ex-husband.

"I'm a survivor of sexual abuse and an 11-year abusive marriage," said Alia, who has only recently begun sharing her story openly. "I'm trying to get used to talking about it publicly. But because of this, I intimately understand the framework of an abusive relationship."

Alia, who has a 15-year track record of working in the community, with special focus in the civil and social rights arena, says her personal experiences have helped frame the way she speaks truth to the world.

"My abuse has given me an understanding of how critical the problem really is, and how devastating it can be," she explained. "There is a domino effect on how abuse affects survivors and the people around them."

Alia said no one knew about the abuse she endured during her marriage and says that she has grown a lot since her traumatic experience.

"The abuse has definitely taught me about empathy on a much higher level," she said. "I've been where a lot of these women have been."

Compounding the religious cultural stigma of openly confronting this issue, Alia said the Muslim community is even more reluctant as a whole from feeling targeted from a national security perspective. She illustrated the reality that Muslims are often negatively targeted as a result of the actions of a tiny minority of deranged criminals and drawing a comparison to African Americans as an example of another targeted community that faces the same or even worse forms of collective profiling and marginalization.

"Members of the community tell me, 'Come on, Sister Alia, why are you trying to make us look bad in the news," she said. "Then, I say, 'Which is worse, us cleaning out the corruption ourselves like we are commanded by God to do, or letting the abusers continue victimizing people because we are afraid of bad press?'"

"But, I tell people it's our job to 'clean house' of these perverts and criminals. And I'll be damned if we have to see another abuse victim on my watch without taking action," said Alia.

The published writer and public speaker spreads her message of action by speaking to community groups around the country about the urgent need to stand against systemic abuse of power. She encourages people of all faiths to visit FaceTogether.org for more information.

"You can't stop an abuser from abusing, and you can't take back abuse once it has happened," she said. "But we can rigorously take steps to limit it from happening again in the future."

Her Advice: "Gently and compassionately encourage survivors to report their abuse because where there is an abuse of power, there is often a higher chance of more victimization."

The Last Word

Collectively, faith communities have to do better in protecting all people from sexual aggression and abuse. People lose faith and churches are divided by abuse, schemes, greed, pride, and all of the other vices that dog faith communities. Some religious communities are beginning to speak out and use #ChurchToo to raise awareness of sexual harassment and violence in social media.

In some cases, it seems that abuse results when church followers begin to elevate their pastors and church leaders to a lofty, god-like pedestal. The fame status that some faith leaders demand or enjoy in our culture feeds the beast of idolatry. We have to be careful not to extend our praise for God to the men or women delivering His word.

Most importantly, we have to confront the wrongs that we see going on around us in our churches and other religious communities. We no longer can afford to go along with the majority or be silent in the face of abuse. We can't care more about the reputation of our church or our faith status than we care about doing the right thing on behalf of victims. And when abusers refuse to listen, we must bring witnesses or use documentation as safeguard methods.

Religious organizations must take the proper steps to prevent inappropriate behavior and abuse. Here are some steps religious organizations can take:

- Vet leaders, volunteers and new hires with a more extensive application and screening process
- Require a criminal background check
- Require and check work and personal reference lists
- Establish a six-month rule before church staff or leaders can work with youth one-on-one
- Encourage the presence of both female and male chaperones or volunteers at church youth functions
- Establish clear rules about touching of minors
- Establish a buddy system with minors on church outings
- Discourage church leaders from facilitating one-on-one meetings in isolated environments

If you are in the midst of an abusive situation, it may be hard to clearly process the big picture without the help of a counselor. Also, it's critical to do something about the abuse by confronting the abuser and immediately removing yourself from the situation. Refer to the resource list in the last chapter to find abuse support. Healing takes time, but it's possible with love and support.

CHAPTER FIVE

A Hostile Work Environment

*"Until there is equity in our industry, with men
and women ... Our community will continue to be a
fertile ground for predators." – Salma Hayek*

Have you faced offensive behavior in the workplace? Although everyone deserves to have a safe and healthy workplace, many women and men are subjected to bullying and abuse every day on the job. Yet, Time Magazine cited a recent poll that 48% of the women who are currently employed in the U.S. report that they have experience sexual, verbal or physical harassment in the workplace. And that figure does not include women who face abuse or harassment outside of work.

"I actually don't think men's behaviors have gotten better," said Hallie Sheffey, who has counseled hundreds of survivors over her four-decade career "I think the current political climate has encouraged people to be more vulgar than they used to be."

Many young women I talk to tell me stories about men who have inappropriately come on to them, and back in the day, there weren't policies and procedures in place when people come forward with complaints. Workplace abuse isn't limited to physical abuse. It can include bullying, jokes, threats, harassment, intimidation, exclusion and assault.

Many survivors of workplace bullying report high levels of stress, helplessness, and hopelessness because others in their workplace see and hear the mistreatment yet choose to do nothing. This communal silence creates a support system for perpetrators, and often allows bullying to carry on for long periods of time.

***

Tanja

Tanja Green has worked in various roles for the public school system in Washington, D.C. In 2015, Tanja did her doctoral dissertation on workplace bullying and found that women are victimized far more often than men. In her research, she learned that 1 in 10 employees are bullied at work, and that statistic has likely grown since then. On a more personal level, she attributes a past miscarriage, anxiety attacks, and excessive stress to past workplace harassment.

"Research on workplace bullying started in the 1990s, but yet some people still believe workplace bullying does not exist," she said. "They dismiss it as whining and disgruntled employees. It's not only real, but in some countries, workplace bullying is illegal."

Tanja said workplace bullying is defined as repeated mistreatment that is deliberate and harmful, either emotionally, verbally or physically.

"I found that workplace bullying commonly occurs in hospitals, schools, and church environments," she explained. "And, if you think about it, that makes sense because power plays a key role in those environments."

Tanja says that just like sexual harassment, workplace bullying and abuse is almost always about a co-worker or manager having power over another person.

"I've seen bullying result in psychological problems, depression, disease, high blood pressure and even suicide attempts," she explained. "One woman I saw even had a massive stroke from harassment at work."

Personally, Tanja shared two past work conflicts where she faced emotional and sexual harassment by men in leadership positions. The first instance occurred while she was working as a special education administrator in Maryland under a difficult principal.

"I found that other employees were watching my every move and reporting back to the principal at my elementary school," she said as she described her toxic work environment. "After I took the job, my principal said: 'I can't *wait* to get with you.' And I let that go in case it was just a slip of the tongue."

However, Tanja sensed that the principal was offended with her because she was happily married and hadn't come on to him like other female employees had. And later, when Tanja told the principal that she had to take three months off for major surgery, he gave her a hard time.

"When I came back to work after my surgery, the locks to my office door were changed, no one would talk to me, someone stole my work keys, and I discovered that someone had shut off the air conditioning to my office only," she said. "But when I went around to other rooms, the air was working just fine."

Later, when Tanja found out that she was pregnant, she intentionally kept the news secret because she feared that someone might try to do something to harm her during her pregnancy.

"But after a couple months, I lost the baby and I think it happened because I was so bogged down with stress from work," Tanja explained. "Around this time, the principal kept sending me memos that said: 'When Are You Quitting??'"

Tanja tried to go to the union president for help in dealing with the harassment, but he took no action on her complaints. And she says the principal got even angrier when she hired an attorney to handle her harassment case.

"In the end, my seven months at that school felt like a lot longer," she said. "It still bothers me that I lost that baby, but I ended up leaving to take a better job in a different school district."

While in another job working as an Individualized Education Plan facilitator, Tanja faced more harassment. A veteran assistant principal in the school district persistently made romantic passes and comments toward her.

"During the very first conversation in his office, he told me, 'People are going to think that we're dating because we're going to be very close. Then he invited me to his house and kept telling me to call him."

When Tanja didn't respond to the assistant principal's repeated advances, he started bad-mouthing her to her supervisor. He even led an attempt to suspend her counseling license. Her effort to file a formal human resources complaint resulted in a brush-off.

"All they did was blame me for having a bad attitude," she said. "The assistant principal kept inviting me over to his house. And he always made derogatory comments like, 'I am expecting you to make a lot of mistakes on the job."

Tanja, now the happy mother of two, stayed on the job as long as she could, but finally resigned after she started experiencing anxiety attacks.

Her Advice: "Stand up for yourself. Some people get very upset when a black woman stands up for herself. They think that we are supposed to accept it when we keep getting abused."

***

Tess

Tess Bernard, who is 63, climbed the ranks of the television business while she worked for NBC in New York. Unfortunately, she recalls a career where she experienced severe verbal abuse, sexual harassment, low self-esteem, and blatant sexism over two decades in the male-dominated industry.

"But prior to that, my very first Me Too experience happened in the late 70's while attending college in New Jersey," said Tess. She recalled, "My major was history and when I ran into my teaching assistant on campus, he asked, 'How come you never came to visit me at my apartment when you received a B in the class?' He then called my classmate's name and said, 'She came to see me and I changed her grade to an A.'"

Tess then asked, "So, if I had paid you a visit, I, too, would have gotten an A? And he said, 'Yes, you certainly would have.' I said, 'No, Thank You! I'm good with this B I actually earned.'"

Tess thought back on the frustrating exchange and told me that There was no way she was going to do anything sexual to boost her grade. She went on to say that back in those days, men wielded all the power and women unfortunately weren't helping each other like they readily do today.

"At one point," Tess recalled, "I worked for a prominent (married) television director who openly told women, 'If you have an affair with me, I'll make your life much easier at work. And many women succumbed to his advances. He clearly had the influence to strongly recommend advancement."

It took a female colleague to point out to Tess that this director was deliberately giving her a hard time simply because she ignored his advances to sleep with him. Tess says she was passed over many times because of her abhorrence to play by his unwritten rules.

"That was the very moment I realized that I was never going to get the promotion I had earnestly worked for and deserved," Tess said. "The men in the TV business were so braggadocios, and it was too much for some women to handle."

Tess also remembers how one secretary from a temp agency never returned to the office after lunch because she couldn't handle all of the sexist remarks and crass behavior by her male colleagues.

"We went through so many head games on the job back then. People often made assumptions that I slept with this guy or that guy at work," she said. "And I hated the fact I could not climb up the corporate ladder because I was smart and worked hard, while my male colleagues with similar attributes were getting promoted.

She recalled instances where managers yelled at her and retaliated against her because she declined sexual invitations from men in powerful corporate positions.

"If I had had the financial means to walk away back then, I would have, and [would have] exposed the truth about the abusive workplace culture," explained Tess, who now works as a freelance communications consultant. "I only wish that there was an attorney today who could go back and file a class action lawsuit on behalf of all the women who endured the sexism that permeated throughout the organization."

Tess regrets not exposing more of the sexist biases that she and other female colleagues faced. Unfortunately, she was always haunted by the adage, "You can't burn bridges." She says a career in television required "very thick skin," and that it was so much tougher than it is today for media professionals because of the implementation of employment discrimination laws.

"As bad as a toxic workplace may seem today for millennials, I can assure you it is tame compared to the tyrannical behavior exhibited in the 1970s and 80s," she stated. "Political correctness was introduced in the 1990s and it took decades for women to finally have a platform to confront their abusers."

Her Advice: "Unfortunately, my generation does not get the recognition for setting the table for what you're now seeing with the #MeToo Movement. Back then, we were silenced, but thankfully women finally have the platform and courage to come forward with their stories and implore them to do so."

The Last Word

The million-dollar question is: Why do some people believe they have a right to bully others in the workplace? Why do some men (and women) feel a sense of entitlement without impunity?

I think the answer is a simple one. Workplace abuse and bullying happens because some manipulators believe they will get away with it. Statistics show that bullying can also come from rivalries at work.

In large part, the onus is on employers to create a work environment where the human resource department is equipped to deal with sexual harassment. There are routine sexual harassment trainings and an environment where all employees feel comfortable speaking out. There is a legal obligation for employers to take every sexual harassment complaint at face value. Managers or human resources professionals should not be weighing whether the claim is true or not, and employees who face bullying and harassment must know that sharing their hardships won't result in retaliation by managers or other employees.

If you currently work in a hostile environment you may be facing unwanted comments, threats, suggestive gestures, inappropriate physical conduct, offered benefits for sexual favors and sexual advances. Facing this behavior can lead to stress, emotional problems, chronic tardiness, excessive absences, the inability to concentrate, and reduced productivity. it's important to develop a toolkit of resources to address the systemic abuse that may include habits to stay safe at work, a go-to ally to escort or accompany you when need be, and a documented routine on how to respond to abuse.

Know your rights! Title VII of the Civil Rights Act of 1964 deemed sexual harassment illegal as a form of gender discrimination. Here are five valuable tips:

Tip #1: Document Everything. Be sure to keep a running file of dates, times and offensive incidents in question. Creating a verifiable track record of your complaints and the responses to them can be invaluable if you have to escalate the problem legally, or at work.

Tip #2: Don't Remain Silent. It's important to communicate that you find the perpetrator's conduct offensive and that it is creating tension. Perhaps the offender is unaware of bad behavior (such as jokes) and you may be able to resolve the problem. Remember, you are NOT powerless!

Tip #3: Detach from Bullying Behavior. Whatever you do, don't stoop to your offender's level and don't do or say anything that you may regret later. Losing your cool may create bigger problems along the way. Be smart about your reactions and the way you handle the harassment!

Tip #4: Know Your Employer's Procedure. Many companies have a documented procedure for handling sexual harassment claims. Ask your human resources representative for a copy of the employer's procedure, and then review it and precisely follow the steps it outlines. If your company doesn't have a harassment procedure, make your supervisor or a higher-level manager aware of the problem.

Tip #5: Pursue Escalation. If you are unable to find resolution at your workplace, don't be afraid to escalate the matter. Typically, the Equal Employment Opportunity Commission or your state's civil rights enforcement agency will investigate your claim and handle the resolution. If the agency is unable to resolve the matter but has deemed your claim valid, it will issue a "Right to Sue" letter. This letter will be valuable ammunition if you choose to file a civil lawsuit for injuries you suffered as a result of the bullying or harassment.

Remember to stand firm in your truth and follow your instinct if you know that you have been unfairly targeted. Resolutions can include: payment for emotional distress, non-monetary benefits, paid legal costs, retroactive pay, job reinstatement (if lost), and most importantly, mandated changes in company policies. Additionally, your victory could help dissuade your harasser in future incidents and send an important message of steep penalties to potential perpetrators and others in the workplace.

CHAPTER SIX

The Abuse of Power

"If Hollywood was a Republican town, Weinstein would still be president, and he'd still be molesting women."
— *Oliver Markus Malloy*

The abuse of power by leaders is only possible when our systems, institutions or citizens uphold violence, turn a blind eye, and allow abuse to go on behind the curtain. Abuse of power or position takes on many different forms, including political corruption, embezzlement, threats of violence and religious abuse. The crux of the abuse of power is built around the idea that people have the right to treat people wrong, break rules, tell lies without repercussions, or even have control over somebody else's body. In fact, many sexual predators operate in support systems that allow them to flourish for years.

In the case of the infamous Harvey Weinstein situation, it was reported that there were women and men strategically placed around the troubled film director who helped set the stage for his predatory practices. His system of henchmen consciously helped cover up decades of abuse and silence more than a dozen survivors in Hollywood.

Communities around the world watched the Weinstein case and dozens of other abuse cases unfold in the following weeks and months. Even Congress joined in the #MeToo flurry as U.S. senators like Claire McCaskill, Mazie Hirono, and Elizabeth Warren began using the hashtag, #MeTooCongress. These brave leaders began sharing personal stories about crude remarks and sexual misconduct they had endured in their careers. It was another example of what the abuse of power looks like in the political arena.

To add to the momentum, congressmen like Blake Farenthold, Trent Franks, John Conyers and Al Franken began to announce their resignations and abrupt decisions not to run for re-election. These and other developments resulted from the mounting weight of harassment cases, new abuse allegations, and public pressure from colleagues and constituents.

The abuse of power is not a new phenomenon, and this type of misconduct touches every area of our society. Earlier this year, I remember seeing CNN's Poppy Harlow interview Supreme Court Justice Ruth Bader Ginsburg. In the interview, Justice Ginsburg, who is 85, recalled how her former chemistry professor at Cornell University attempted to use his position to coerce her into having sex in order to get a higher grade in the class.

"My professor said, 'I'll give you a practice exam,' but actually he was asking for sex," Ginsburg explained. "I understood what he was asking for and I said, 'How dare you!'"

After she rejected his invitation for sex, Ginsburg said she knew getting a 100% grade on her exam was out of the question. "Back then, we didn't have a name for [that behavior] but some people would say, 'Boys will be boys,'" Ginsburg said. "Sexual harassment was often dismissed as, 'She made it up,' or 'She's too thin-skinned.'"

The law scholar expressed her support for the #MeToo Movement and what the implications could mean for women in the future. "It's amazing to me that, for the first time, women are being listened to," she said. "I think this [movement] is very healthy … [The problem] is too widespread."

There is a very long list of notable leaders that I could discuss on this subject. However, in this chapter, we will explore the abuse of power of a world-renowned spiritual leader who was followed by millions. You'll meet two women who reveal personal accounts about Maharishi Mahesh Yogi, the Indian monk from the 1960s who famously served as a spiritual guru to the Beatles. These stories share two insider views of a man who touted his celibacy and the celibacy of others as the way to achieve enlightenment, while he himself had numerous sexual affairs.

***

Judith

Judith Bourque is widely acknowledged as the first woman to come out publicly to admit that Maharishi actually had sexual relationships with women. Like many other #MeToo stories, many of the followers of this wealthy and powerful spiritual leader questioned the truth of these relationships.

Whether we talk about President Clinton, Bill Cosby, or a Hindu monk, there are parallels when it comes to some larger-than-life figures and the power they possess and abuse. But like every true story in this book, Judith's story is very compelling. She shares intimate details of her romance with Maharishi as well as the bumps and jerks of being a member of the internationally famed Guru's inner circle for two years.

Judith, a 22-year-old Catholic from Boston, had started meditating two years prior to beginning Maharishi's three-month teacher training course. She headed to India to become one of his meditation teachers in January of 1970, much to her parents' dismay. She would eventually become the spiritual leader's sexual partner ... a role she was not prepared for.

"I thought I was going to be meeting something like a modern-day Jesus, a living prophet," Judith said about her expectations before their first interaction. So, she was very surprised when the celibate monk began showing a romantic interest in her. And like any admirer, he showered her with special attention, nice clothing, and jewelry.

"I felt chosen by my guru (my god), so I wasn't about to push him or his advances away," Judith explained of their mutual love. "But that's the way a charismatic cult leader will often work if he wants to manipulate a disciple."

Sexually, it was obvious that Maharishi was not an experienced lover, Judith explained about the shocking experience. "At 52, I believe it was his first time going all the way," Judith said. She recalled that Maharishi had even asked what her private part was called during her secret visit to his room.

"Don't tell anyone," he told her, and Judith agreed, as it could cause a stir among his closest devotees. But soon others in Maharishi's circle did take note of the way he fussed over Judith.

Eventually Judith learned of Maharishi's other sexual partners within his close circle of devotees. Later, she took notice of the way he began excessively charging $1,000,000 for his private "enlightenment program."

"I felt like he had gone off the deep end," Judith recalled. "He was claiming to be this celibate monk and was never honest about that. He even advised some married couples to practice celibacy. If a spiritual leader advises a code of behavior but practices another, disciples become both hurt and confused."

In 1968, Actress Mia Farrow claimed that Maharishi groped her during a private meeting with him at his ashram in India. The incident publicly hurt the guru's image and news of the assault diminished his following.

"Sex and money can be so many people's downfall," Judith said. "And it was Maharishi's, too. I think he developed a taste for sex and then just basically did whatever he wanted."

Judith also observed first-hand how Hinduism was not a religion that fostered gender equality. As a Hindu monk and the creator of the Transcendental Meditation movement, Maharishi called the shots about everything.

"I definitely saw an abuse of power with Maharishi," Judith remarked from a position of having witnessed much of what went on behind the scenes. "There was so much dishonesty. I didn't like that the movement was very male-dominated."

After two years, Judith was finally clear that life with Maharishi would only lead to greater unhappiness. She left him and his movement, never to return. She moved to Sweden to be with her future life partner. Now a widow, she currently lives in Stockholm near her son and grandchildren.

Maharishi, who died at age 91 in 2008, left a reported $11 billion in his estate at the time of death. Judith said, "I did not feel a lot of emotion when he died, having let go of him many, many years ago."

Judith is now a filmmaker and holistic therapist, and says she shares her story so others can use it as a warning sign for young women who are seeking a spiritual teacher. But she also shares it to reveal cultic aspects of spiritual movements.

"Telling the truth about my relationship with this man has been such a tremendous relief on so many levels," she wrote in her book, *Robes of Silk, Feet of Clay.* "I am absolutely sure it was the right thing to do ... It was time to let go of the denial."

Her Advice: Eventually forgiving needs to be a part of any hurtful experience in order to move on with one's life, but it's also important to be able to distinguish between forgiving and condoning.

***

Susan

Like Judith, Dr. Susan Shumsky was also in Maharishi Mahesh Yogi's inner circle of followers in the 1970s. Susan, a self-proclaimed flower child, was one of the famous Hindu leader's personal attendants. Of Susan's 22 years living at the leader's ashrams, she spent six of those serving on his personal staff. A month before she learned Transcendental Meditation, she moved away from the recreational drugs of her hippie past, like LSD. She never took them again.

"Transcendental Meditation saved my life," Susan said, but she also recalled how the mounting sexual claims against the self-professed celibate monk caused many devotees to begin asking questions. "I have personally talked to at least four women who've had sex with Maharishi, and they definitely didn't make up their stories."

Susan said she started hearing about Maharishi's sexual relationships in the 1970s, including Mia Farrow's claim that he had made a move on her.

"As far as I know, all of the women who slept with him had consensual sex," said Susan, who contends the guru never made a pass at her. "To many, Maharishi was almost god-like, so somewhat gullible women may have easily succumbed to a powerful man like him."

In addition to having an insider's view of how Maharishi used and abused power, Susan had her own power struggle in the 1980s with a businessman who inappropriately propositioned her. His crude behavior cost Susan thousands of dollars in lost business revenue.

"For 20 years I worked as a freelance jewelry designer in New York City, and my major client was Meyer's Jewelry," she said. "My jewelry design buyer retired and a new guy was hired to take his place."

This leadership change proved to be a tough adjustment for Susan when she discovered the man was sexist.

"The new buyer told me he wanted to get together over dinner for a supposed meeting," Susan explained. "After the meeting he suggested we go to his place. Then he threatened me and abruptly stopped doing business with me because I didn't play along with him."

When Susan reached out to the president of Meyer's Jewelry, she was stunned that he refused to do anything about it. He didn't contact the buyer, confront him, or even apologize. When she suggested that the buyer be fired for misconduct, the company president told her that would never happen.

"This was the 1980s, when there were no sexual harassment lawsuits," said Susan. "It was unbelievable that I had no recourse. I just had to swallow it and move on to some other way to make a living."

Susan did just that. She is now a best-selling author. Her latest book, *Maharishi & Me,* was released in February, and she has written 13 others. She has spent 50 years teaching people about meditation, intuition, and affirmation. Susan has dedicated her life to helping people take command of their lives in powerful, positive ways.

The Last Word

In many ways, corruption seems to be the norm and not the exception when it comes to all leadership. (Have you watched the news lately?) Some people say abuse of power is the biggest problem our society faces today.

The abuse of power has both big and small implications that cause greater harm: People are disillusioned, business is lost, funds disappear, jobs are lost, and people are killed. In order to unveil abuse of power in various arenas, it starts with each of us. First, you have to pay close attention to what's going on around you. Stay up on the news, read as much as you can, and interact with other folks to stay better informed. Whether the abuse comes from the dominant influence of social media giants, workplace politics, government collusion, religious abuse and the like, when you don't approve of what you see happening, ask these questions:

- Who has the power?

- What is the system of power?

- What are their objectives?

- What are the outcomes?

Thanks to many movements (like the #MeToo Movement), and in order to grow in political activism, people are increasingly using their voices against abuse of all kinds. Raising your voice is the only way things will change at every level.

CHAPTER SEVEN

Men Are Survivors, Too

"We must send a message across the world that there is no disgrace in being a survivor of sexual violence. The shame is on the aggressor." -Angelina Jolie

Unfortunately, a double standard exists in society when it comes to male survivors of sexual abuse. It seems that, to some extent, the #MeToo Movement has forgotten to include male survivors. Although abuse happens less often with men than with women, men and boys are indeed subjected to domestic or sexual violence. In a 2013 National Crime Victimization survey of 40,000 U.S. households, 38% reported incidents of rape and sexual violence committed against men.

Although about 3% (or 1 in 33) of American men have experienced an attempted or completed rape in their lifetime, there seems to be a broad misunderstanding that the conversation about male survivors somehow diminishes the focus on female survivors.

In 2017, actor Terry Crews shared a memory of being assaulted by entertainment agent Adam Bennett. The well-known and powerful agent represents stars such as Adam Sandler, Sylvester Stallone, and Eddie Murphy. Crews reported an account at a party where Bennett assaulted him by grabbing his genitals and taunting him sexually. Following the incident, Crews filed a police report and pursued legal action. In a Good Morning America interview, Crews claimed that there is an abuse of power in Hollywood. He also said that he understood why many women stay silent after facing harassment.

"It's like being a prisoner of war and you're trying to think about what's the best time to come out," Crews explained passionately. "And a lot of people just don't understand and end up blaming the victim. And I've said I will not be shamed. What kind of man would I be to tell my kids that if someone touches you where you don't want to be touched, to tell someone, and then I don't do it. I knew instantly that I had to tell my story so that other people could be freed."

Crews is in good company of male Hollywood actors who have bravely talked about sexual misconduct. This includes *Mummy* star Brendan Fraser, and *Star Trek* actor Anthony Rapp. They shared incidents of butt pinching, crude jokes, sexual advances and inappropriate touching.

Statistics show that due to shame, societal biases and a lack of compassion, men are much less likely to report abuse because they often are afraid they won't be taken seriously or will be told to "be tough." There are also assumptions that men couldn't possibly be abused by women. The graphic below shares more statistics about male survivors.

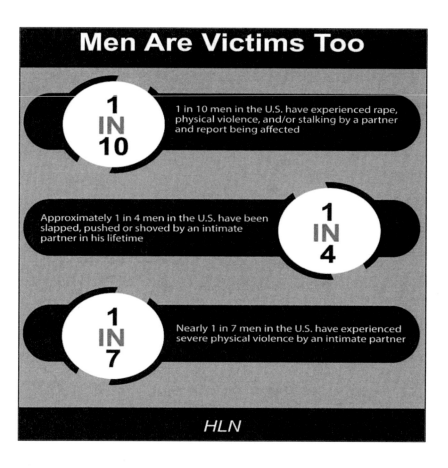

***

Conny

Conny Larsson is an internationally known Swedish author, actor, and meditation teacher who was also active in Maharishi's meditation movement in the 1960s and 1970s. Conny also followed Sathya Sai Baba, another Hindu monk who drew followers from around the world. During Conny's tenure working for Sai Baba's organization, he learned what abuse of power looked like from close range. Conny was abused by the renowned guru. However, his abuse didn't start there. He also suffered sexual abuse early in his life at age 4.

Growing up with an alcoholic father, Conny would often witness his dad abuse his helpless and loving mother. When Fridays would roll around, Conny knew it meant his dad would have money to buy alcohol and his mother would disappear to avoid his father's alcohol-driven beatings. Fridays also meant that his father would invite his boss over because they were drinking buddies.

"My father's boss lived on the next floor of our apartment building and he would come over to drink until Dad would be knocked out," Conny recalled. "It was then when he would sexually abuse me, and this went on from age 4 up to age 10."

Conny never blamed his long-suffering mother for her absence because he knew the severity of abuse she faced at his father's hands. Although it was a topic not discussed, Conny believes that his older brother may also have been sexually abused by the terrifying boss he nicknamed "The Visitor."

"The sound of a man's voice being raised in an angry tone caused me to crawl into my shell," said Conny. "Occasionally, Dad would try to force feed me. He shoved the spoon [of food] in my mouth until my gums bled, and Mom shouted at him to stop until she was hoarse."

As a result of the sexual, physical and emotional abuse, Conny went mute for a few years. In that time, he used only his smiles to communicate with others and mask the pain he endured as a child.

"I would break away from [Dad's] grasp and withdraw to one of the places where I used to hide from grown-ups," said Conny. He credits his Sunday school teacher for helping him eventually break his silence. "I was always the first pupil to be there every Sunday morning and the last to leave after the lessons."

But Conny lost faith both in Jesus and his Protestant faith as he "could not understand why Jesus did not help me." As he grew older, he felt "abandoned by the truth and the light."

While in acting school, Conny saw an article promoting an event where Maharishi would be lecturing in various locations around Sweden. Conny attended the event and felt a divine calling to follow "His Holiness."

Like many faithful European and American followers amid the 1960s revolution, Conny moved to India on a quest for spiritual enlightenment. He later became a transcendental meditation teacher and rose through the ranks to work closely with Maharishi.

"I worked for Maharishi as a personal secretary," Conny said. "My co-secretary was the famous American author, John Gray. John was there even before me and we grew to be good friends."

In 1978, Conny began following another guru named Sathya Sai Baba. Sai Baba was an avatar, a god-like figure living "an exemplary" life as a monk. He gained spiritual followers and international notoriety after performing "miraculous" healings and resurrections. It wasn't until years later that Conny would deem the spiritual leader and his cult a fraud.

"One day Sai Baba chose me to come up to his private interview room," said Conny, who recalled being invited to visit and meditate with the spiritual leader in his early 30s. There was a total of 10 visits before the sexual assault began. "He [Sai Baba] was grooming me. I felt like 'Conny the holy one' because I was chosen from all of the others. Then he started to masturbate. And then one day he began taking my pants down."

Conny says that Sai Baba used his position and his larger-than-life presence to sexually exploit him, along with other men and boys.

"Imagine being chosen to be almost a god figure. He had a palace, dressed in white robes, and stood at the top of his terrace to greet hundreds of followers every day," Conny explained. "But really, he was the devil himself. ... I think that he was gay from Day One but just hid behind his monk title."

At his peak, Sai Baba controlled over a thousand spiritual centers in 130 countries. His powerful Sathya Sai Organization did and still does run hospitals, orphanages, schools, and centers. Conny ran one of the orphanages for years, until he discovered Sai Baba was a pedophile and was having sex with some of the boys.

"I never stopped being a whistle-blower," said Conny, who faced threats and danger for publicly speaking out negatively about the spiritual leader who died in 2011. "Sai Baba used manipulation and the innocence of his believers to get what he wanted."

Despite experiencing so much abuse, the Swedish citizen is currently thriving as a popular author and speaker. He is currently working on his next book.

"I faced abuse of power, abuse of life, and manipulation," said Conny, who is the author of *The Beatles Maharishi and I,* and *Behind the Clown's Mask.""*The [gurus] were very good spiritual teachers in terms of meditation techniques, but they were living a lie."

His Advice: "I know so many men who were abused by older women. But when men are abused, they don't come out about it. They have to come out of silence, just like the women do."

***

Eric

Eric Schumacher is an award-winning and critically acclaimed actor, director and producer. He has played a lot of tough guy characters in film and television, but he has a very different story to share about his brush with sexual harassment. When the survivor is a heterosexual man, like Eric, he says "submitting an account about another guy hitting on you at work really isn't the most comfortable thing for most men to do."

"As a teenager in school, I had a variety of retail jobs in order to make ends meet," said Eric. "My manager at the time was physically much bigger than me, both very tall and very wide."

Eric was the youngest employee at the store. He had begun to notice that of all of the employees, his twenty-something boss seemed to only be focused on him.

"He started making sexually suggestive comments all the time and blowing kisses at me at work," Eric recalled. "He never touched me, but his attitude toward me definitely made me feel like I was in danger."

Eric said the awkward advances went on for over six months, and would only occur when they were alone. The unwanted attention caused him to question his manliness and masculinity at a time when he was already awkward.

"I wasn't gay and I wasn't interested, yet every day my boss was making me very uncomfortable. I was conflicted between what would make me seem weak and what I should do to protect myself," he said. "The flirting was making me angrier and angrier but I didn't know what I could or should do about it. So, I said nothing."

Powerlessness is reported to be a common response when a person with power or authority shows sexually aggressive behavior. Eric said he never thought about escalating the incidents to a district manager because he almost never saw the district manager at the store.

"I never received training on how to address this kind of thing," he said. "I really didn't feel like there was anything I could do. And if I did talk, I was afraid I would lose my job."

The harassment abruptly stopped when Eric's manager began talking about his new girlfriend. The manager eventually married the woman and appeared to be genuinely in love.

"I remember that I kept telling myself that I was making too much of a fuss about my boss," said Eric, who is now happily married and has since studied martial arts and self-defense. "Looking back, I should have confronted him immediately. I would have said. 'I'm not interested in you in that way and this is not the way to treat someone at a job site,' and made sure that there were witnesses around when I said it."

Eric often blogs at ericschumacherfilm.com, and is passionate about supporting survivors of sexual abuse. He believes that it is everyone's responsibility to speak out against gender inequalities as well.

"This issue is close to my heart," said Eric. "When I've taught self-defense classes, I would hear a lot of stories about what women face. I have a lot of friends who are survivors of sexual assault and it infuriates me that they've had to deal with this. In the entertainment industry, I've so far been blessed to work with mostly very good folk in very supportive environments, but I know of a couple of incidents that were utterly unacceptable."

His Advice: "The #MeToo Movement is an important dialogue. We have to figure out how we must make sexual assault and true sexual harassment much harder to get away with, and we have to empower people to speak out when there's a real issue. We need to educate those segments of society that don't understand the issue, and we need to stand up for each other. I also believe that everyone should learn to defend themselves physically. It's hard to emphasize enough how empowering that can be, to know that you're not helpless if you have to take a stand."

The Last Word

Victimized men and boys need to be taken seriously and feel a greater sense of safety when reporting abuse. Equally as important, men should NOT feel as though reporting abuse threatens their masculinity.

"I can remember one male client that I had who was embarrassed to report that he was battered," said Hallie Sheffey, the seasoned therapist from West Michigan. "He would try to tiptoe around his wife not to set her off. But that was impossible because you never know what will shift someone to set off mode."

Unfortunately, when the police are called about an altercation, they almost always automatically think the male is at fault — especially when the man is black, Sheffey said.

"Another client had his front teeth knocked out by his girlfriend," Sheffey said. "He didn't bother to fight back because he didn't want to go to jail for defending himself. There is definitely a double standard."

Although it's hard to believe, the Federal Bureau of Investigation only updated its official definition of forcible rape in 2012. The new definition of forcible rape was changed to remove female language and degenderize it to include male victims. The old definition referenced "a female" and "her," while the new language references "the victim." This is important because this definition is used to describe and categorize national crime statistics. This gender agnostic definition has impact on data reporting by state governments, too.

National organizations like Men Can Stop Rape and 1 in 6 advocate for education, mentoring and support for men and male survivors. Everyone must be more cognizant that male children, male inmates, and other male populations are vulnerable to rape and abuse. No one deserves to be sexually assaulted or coerced, and both men and women should have access to resources and a pathway to healing.

CONCLUSION
What Do We Do Now?

It has been one of the greatest privileges of my life to interview and get to know the survivors featured in this book. I'm proud to say that some are now my friends. My biggest takeaway from interviewing over 20 survivors has been a better grasp on the devastating effect of harassment and abuse.

There is no question in my mind that every single experience I've documented is true. Each survivor has authentically shared their feelings of pain and shame.

Surprisingly, this book revealed another survivor who is close to home — my mom. Through our discussions about this book, my mom, Bonita, shared how her uncle molested her when she was 9 years old.

"My aunt hadn't even gotten around the corner when Uncle Jimmy jumped into bed with me during an overnight visit to their home," my mom said. "He had taken off his pants and pulled my covers back to fondle me. It was only God who gave me the presence of mind to jump out of bed and lock myself in their bathroom."

She said, from that day forward it changed her relationship with him and her aunt who hadn't learned of his continuous sexual advances till years later.

"Around the age of 16 I finally got the confidence to tell my aunt and my mom," my mother said. "He was always trying to get quick feels and eventually I started avoiding my aunt because of him."

She said the stories of the survivors in this book inspired her to share her own story so that parents reading it can be alert of the signs of molestation.

"Abusers like my uncle will always lie and deny," she said. "But parents still need to be vigilant because you really can't trust many people these days."

After six months of research and interviews, I've gleaned that everyone truly does have a story to share. The #MeToo Movement is not just a cultural fad or the latest bandwagon women are hopping on. The stories that are finally seeing light — and more importantly, the results of the told stories — are revealing a gargantuan problem, and some solutions, too.

I'm grateful that people are listening and BELIEVING survivors in a bigger way. And with more believers, many institutions are changing or developing protocol to deal with abuse and its perpetrators. Here's another look at statistics that depict the magnitude of this societal problem.

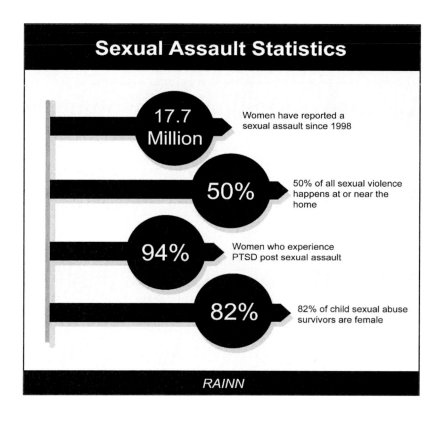

Sexual Assault Statistics

17.7 Million — Women have reported a sexual assault since 1998

50% — 50% of all sexual violence happens at or near the home

94% — Women who experience PTSD post sexual assault

82% — 82% of child sexual abuse survivors are female

RAINN

So, where do we go from here? Well, with more believers, more institutions are changing or developing protocol to deal with abuse and its perpetrators. Finally, we are seeing more apologies (albeit late!), more lost contracts and business, and also more convictions for old abuse claims. It feels like a heavy cloak of darkness is being lifted. This new momentum has also been resulting in broken and hurting survivors coming out of the closet.

We are also seeing more convictions for old abuse cases. In April 2018, iconic entertainer Bill Cosby was convicted on three counts of sexual assault. The 80-year-old faces up to 10 years in prison for each count. It's the only criminal case to get traction from a barrage of allegations from more than 60 women who say the famous TV dad drugged, molested or raped them. In the same week of Cosby's conviction, new accusations arose against former NBC news anchor Tom Brokaw. Thus, the trend of abuse allegations and revelations continues.

Silent Majority

When people are bullied and abused, they often lose their voice and remain silent about their feelings and their rights. Many have just gone along and have forgotten that they have the right to say "No." Through the years, many women have refrained from speaking out about their abuse because of fear: fear of rejection, fear of retaliation, fear of being blamed, and fear of not being believed.

Many survivors I interviewed still worry that their perpetrator's bad behavior will be minimized or brushed off. But the #MeToo Movement has provided a pathway for the silent majority to share their experiences and unity in big and small ways.

Even as I publish this book, I recognize that many survivors will never be able to freely raise their hand about their abuse. Some still live in danger of being attacked, sued, smeared, or even killed for telling the truth. But I view every brave voice as a small victory and progress.

The Stages of Grief

1	2	3	4	5
DENIAL	**ANGER**	**BARGAINING**	**DEPRESSION**	**ACCEPTANCE**
"This can't be happening" or "They can't be happening."	"Why is this happeing to me? Who is at fault?	"Maybe if I just do ..."	"I'm too sad to deal with my reality"	"I am at peace with what has happened"

There is value in sharing the Five Stages of Grief for those who may be quietly coping with abuse and its aftermath. The stages of grief often occur as a result of abuse, trauma, illness, loss or death. These stages are commonly used to evaluate one's feelings and understanding about the grieving process. It's valuable for survivors to identify their own current stage of grief as they react to traumatic experiences internally, or when they wear their emotions on their sleeve. Experts say not all people experience these stages in the same order, but this is normal.

Stage 1: Denial is a defense mechanism that can occur when survivors are numb regarding their emotions. It is a temporary response to get the survivor through the initial pain they've experienced.

Stage 2: Anger helps survivors mask feelings of denial and isolation. The anger in this stage is typically directed toward the person who caused them pain. It is sometimes directed toward anyone around the survivor.

Stage 3: Bargaining is the result of feelings of helplessness, guilt and vulnerability. These "if only" thoughts are another defense to accepting painful realities.

Stage 4: Depression is a stage of sadness and regret. The implications of the reality begin to set in as many survivors separate themselves from their loved ones. Comfort is a helpful remedy.

Stage 5: Acceptance is the final stage that not everyone experiences. It is not a stage of happiness, but rather a time of calm and withdrawal.

Coping with abuse is a personal experience, and it's comforting to provide support for those who may be going through these stages. This process is a part of the healing process.

It is progress that many survivors are being freed of the burden that their abuse has caused them. Some are joining support groups and other silence breakers are pursuing legal action. That's why I don't agree that the #MeToo Movement should be broadly labeled as "going too far."

Have We Gone Too Far?

I recognize that some men and women have blasted the #MeToo Movement, saying survivors and accusations have gone too far. Many have criticized survivors for the delay in reporting abuse, and for "jumping on the bandwagon" to destroy some men's careers.

Some people blame the movement for curtailing innocent interactions between men and women, particularly in work environments. Critics allege that some men are "frightened" to speak or touch for fear of being labeled as a sexual predator.

I completely agree that when allegations arise, there needs to be an investigative process and proof to discourage unfair defamation. Survivors should be expected to verify their claims.

Is there a chance that some allegations are untrue? Of course. However, overall, the movement is a small victory for a longtime, deep-rooted problem. I recognize that social media has created a platform for news to travel fast about sexual harassment allegations, but the vast majority of those coming out have spoken with conviction, and oftentimes have provided witnesses and proof. Thus, more good than bad has resulted from the movement.

And, remember that one progressive offshoot from the 2017 movement has been the Time's Up Initiative.

The Time's Up Initiative

The Time's Up Initiative is a concerted effort to fight against sexual harassment and promote equity in the workplace. The name refers to a hypothetical clock that shows that time is running out on the days where women will continue accepting sexual abuse. It was founded on January 1, 2018 by a group of Hollywood celebrities, including actress Rose McGowan. If you'd like to learn more about this movement, check out McGowan's book, Brave.

Since its inception, the Time's Up Initiative has raised more than $21 million for the Legal Defense Fund and has gathered more than 200 volunteer lawyers. The fund will defray legal and public relations costs in select cases of those who have experienced sexual harassment and retaliation. The legal and financial momentum behind the effort seeks equal representation, opportunities, pay equity, and greater representation of women of color, immigrant women, disabled women, and lesbian, bisexual, and transgendered women who struggle for a fair shake in the workforce.

Over the past year, many celebrities have made sizable donations and have shown support by attending award shows like the Grammys, the Oscars and the Golden Globes with a dress code to show solidarity and unity among women in attendance. The initiative has been one more way that women and survivors have organized in a positive manner.

"Women have been silent for so long and these movements are overdue," said Hallie Sheffey, who worked with many survivors as a therapist in West Michigan for four decades. "But, I don't think we have created a mechanism for men to come forward, come clean and still be safe."

Sheffey referenced the long list of high-profile accusers who have all either lost their jobs, been persecuted, or been publicly shamed. She contends that, "We need to attempt to create a way for men to come clean after they have had a change of heart or reformed. I wonder if there is a way for men to acknowledge that they now see things through a different lens, yet not be blamed by their own omission."

4 Ways to Support a Survivor

Whether we know it or not, we all have survivors of sexual violence and harassment in our families and close circle. I feel it is critically important to end this section by sharing four constructive ways each of us can show comfort to a survivor. Your words, prayers, kind gestures, resources, and compassion can greatly assist a survivor with healing.

I would also like to add that if YOU are the survivor, seeking professional help is likely the best form of self-care. Some survivors say that a part of them died when they were abused. If you can relate to this analogy, you should also know that death is something that needs to be dealt with. Here are four methods to share comfort:

Offer a Listening Ear. Every survivor has a story or two to share. Offering a listening ear may inspire them to seek safety, get counseling, and avoid isolation. Just spending time out of your day to call them or meet them in person may play an important role in the healing process.

Validate Their Story. One of the most hurtful responses is when a survivor isn't believed. Or worse, when a survivor is blamed for the abuse. There is never an excuse to blame a victim. Also, never respond to a survivor by saying, "I know how you feel," because each person's experience is unique. However, you can respond by saying, "I'm here if you need me," or something of that nature.

Provide Resources. Asking a survivor what you can do to support them demonstrates love and could help them avoid feeling of hopelessness. If you can't personally help them in any way, you can provide helpful contacts or direct them to where they can find much-needed resources.

Embrace Self-Care. Survivor stories can be traumatic, even for supporters. Listening to or supporting a survivor can be a long and draining process. There are times when it is appropriate to take a step back to avoid getting consumed by the survivor's hardships. Know when to embrace self-care in order to stay emotionally and psychologically healthy. This helps the survivor also, because if you are mentally healthy, you will be more motivated to show them support.

Finally, I'd like to leave you with one challenge: Think of ways you can be more conscientious after reading these powerful survivor stories. Here is a memorable quote regarding the #MeToo Movement from Tarana Burke, the #MeToo Founder: "After this moment is gone, we have to continue these conversations and start talking about what community healing looks like ... I think survivors will be in the forefront of that effort."

RESOURCES FOR SURVIVORS

Where do you turn if you're facing unwanted abuse or a life-threatening situation? One of the most common responses from the survivors interviewed for this book was that they lacked resources and support. Many survivors shared that they didn't know who to talk and that they felt alone. This feedback impressed upon me the need for a chapter dedicated to resources for survivors.

"We can never assume that a person CAN always protect themselves from abuse," explained Sheffey. "In some instances, that may not be possible. Like when a woman gets raped after she's been drinking."

Sheffey went on to say some women ask for help from professionals like her while still keeping the abuse private.

"A lot of times, women would tell me that their sister or friend was in an abusive situation, when they really were asking for help [for] themselves. And the important thing is to empower the victim to do whatever they want to do about their situation."

But Sheffey also explained that many female victims shy away from reporting abuse to avoid being labeled as a troublemaker in their community.

"Some women are not raised to be empowered to speak up about abuse," she said. "A lot of people don't want to speak out and ruffle any feathers, so they just stay silent."

However, once survivors stand up to a predator, they often change their behavior. Sheffey said, "It's a good thing regarding the trend of women raising their voices about their stories."

Develop a Safety Plan

It can be extremely dangerous and difficult to leave an abusive relationship. The National Domestic Violence Hotline and many other organizations encourage survivors to create a safety plan during and after a toxic relationship. Over 70% of domestic violence murders occur after the relationship ends because in this stage, the abuser has nothing left to lose.

Thus, safety plans can be critical to outline vital information needed for a variety of outcomes to the escape process. A safety plan provides clarity for the survivor and for the family of the survivor. The plan helps survivors to ensure they have emotional support as they transition to a safer place. Safety plans can include details about how to keep children and pets safe as well as how to stay safe when pregnant.

Safety plans include:

- How to get out of a house safely
- Identifying safe places
- How to inform your support network of your status
- How to safely store weapons
- Ways to keep your children safe
- Teaching children how to call 911

There are numerous organizations that offer online resources and support for women and men facing domestic abuse. I must credit survivor Dana Carter's organization, Precious Pearls Ministry, for this comprehensive resource guide. It is included to ensure that victims can get support.

National Sexual Assault
Hotline, Rape, Abuse &
Incest National Network
(800) 656-HOPE (4673)
 www.rainn.org
(site offers live chat)

The National Domestic
Violence Hotline
(800) 799-7233
 www.thehotline.org

The National Organization
for Men Against Sexism
(720) 466-3882
 www.nomas.org

Alabama Coalition Against
Domestic Violence
P.O. Box 4762
Montgomery, AL 36101
(334) 832-4842 or (800)
650-6522
 www.acadv.org

Alaska Network on
Domestic
and Sexual Violence
130 Seward Street,
Room 209
Juneau, AK 99801
(907) 586-3650
 www.andvsa.org

Arizona Coalition Against
Domestic Violence
2800 N. Central Ave.,
Suite 1570
Phoenix, AZ 85004
(602) 279-2900 or
(800) 782-6400
 www.azcadv.org
Email: acadv@azadv.org

Arkansas Coalition Against
Domestic Violence
1401 W. Capitol Avenue,
Suite 170
Little Rock, AR 72201
(501) 907-5612 or
(800) 269-4668
www.domesticpeace.com
kbangert@domesticpeace.com

California Partnership to
End
Domestic Violence
P.O. Box 1798
Sacramento, CA 95812
(916) 444-7163 or (800)
524-4765
 www.cpedv.org
Email: info@cpedv.org

Colorado Coalition Against
Domestic Violence
P. O. Box 18902
Denver, CO 80218
(303) 831-9632 or
(888) 788-7091
 www.ccadv.org

Connecticut Coalition
Against
Domestic Violence
90 Pitkin Street
East Hartford, CT 06108
(860) 282-7899
(800) 281-1481 In State
www.ctcadv.org
Email: info@ctcadv.org

Delaware Coalition Against
Domestic Violence
100 W. 10th Street, #703
Wilmington, DE 19801
(302) 658-2958 or
(800) 701-0456
www.dcadv.org
Email: dcadv@dcadv.org

DC Coalition Against
Domestic Violence
1718 P Street, Suite T-6
Washington, DC 20036
(202) 299-1181
www.dccadv.org
Email: help@dccadv.org

Florida Coalition Against
Domestic Violence
425 Office Plaza
Tallahassee, FL 32301
(850) 425-2749 or
(800) 500-1119
www.fcadv.org

Georgia Coalition Against
Domestic Violence
114 New Street #B
Decatur GA 30030
(404) 209-0280
www.gcadv.org

Hawaii State Coalition
Against Domestic Violence
716 Umi Street, Suite 210
Honolulu, HI 96819-2337
(808) 832-9316
www.hscadv.org

Idaho Coalition Against
Sexual & Domestic Violence
815 Park Boulevard, #140
Boise, ID 83712
(208) 384-0419 or
(888) 293-6118
www.idvsa.org
domvio@mindspring.com

Illinois Coalition Against
Domestic Violence
801 S. 11th Street
Springfield, IL 62703
(217) 789-2830
www.ilcadv.org
ilcadv@ilcadv.org

Indiana Coalition Against
Domestic Violence
1915 W. 18th Street
Indianapolis, IN 46202
(800) 332-7385
www.violenceresource.org

Iowa Coalition Against
Domestic Violence
515 28th Street, #104
Des Moines, IA 50312
(800) 942-0333
 www.icadv.org

Kansas Coalition
Against Sexual
and Domestic Violence
634 SW Harrison Street
Topeka, KS 66603
(785) 232-9784
www.kcsdv.org
Email: coalition@kcsdv.org

Kentucky Domestic
Violence Association
P.O. Box 356
Frankfort, KY 40602
(502) 209-5381
 www.kdva.org

Louisiana Coalition Against
Domestic Violence
P.O. Box 77308
Baton Rouge, LA 70879
(225) 752-1296
 www.lcadv.org

Maine Coalition to End
Domestic Violence
170 Park Street
Bangor, ME 04401
(207) 941-1194
www.mcedv.org
info@mcedv.org

Maryland Network Against
Domestic Violence
6911 Laurel-Bowie Road,
Bowie, MD 20715
(301) 352-4574 or
(800) 634-3577
 www.mnadv.org
mnadv@aol.com

Jane Doe,
Inc./Massachusetts
Coalition Against Sexual
Assault and
Domestic Violence
14 Beacon Street, #507
Boston, MA 02108
(617) 248-0922
TTY/TTD (617) 263-2200
 www.janedoe.org
info@janedoe.org

Michigan Coalition
Against Domestic
& Sexual Violence
3893 Okemos Road, #B-2
Okemos, MI 48864
(517) 347-7000
www.mcadsv.org
general@mcadsv.org

Minnesota Coalition for
Battered Women
1821 University Avenue
West, #S-112
St. Paul, MN 55104
(800) 289-6177
 www.mcbw.org

Mississippi Coalition
Against
Domestic Violence
P.O. Box 4703
Jackson, MS 39296
(601) 981-9196
www.mcadv.org

Missouri Coalition Against
Domestic Violence
718 East Capitol Avenue
Jefferson City, MO 65101
(573) 634-4161
www.mocadv.org
mcadv@sockets.net

Montana Coalition Against
Domestic
& Sexual Violence
P.O. Box 818
Helena, MT 59624
(406) 443-7794 or
(888) 404-7794
www.mcadsv.com
mcadsv@mt.net

Nebraska Domestic
Violence
and Sexual Assault
Coalition
1000 O Street, #102
Lincoln, NE 68508
(402) 476-6256
(877) 215-0167 Spanish
In State
www.ndvsac.org
info@ndvsac.org

Nevada Network Against
Domestic Violence
220 S. Rock Blvd. Suite 7,
Reno, NV 89502-2355
(775) 828-1115 or
(800) 500-1556
www.nnadv.org

New Hampshire Coalition
Against Domestic and
Sexual Violence
P.O. Box 353
Concord, NH 03302
(603) 224-8893
(866) 644-3574 In State
www.nhcadsv.org

New Jersey Coalition for
Battered Women
1670 Whitehorse Hamilton
Square
Trenton, NJ 08690
(609) 584-8107 or
(800) 572-7233
www.njcbw.org
info@njcbw.org

New Mexico State Coalition
Against Domestic Violence
200 Oak NE, #4
Albuquerque, NM 87106
(505) 246-9240
(800) 773-3645 In State
www.nmcadv.org

New York State Coalition
Against Domestic Violence
350 New Scotland Avenue
Albany, NY 12054
(518) 482-5464
 (800) 942-6908 Spanish-
In State
www.nyscadv.org
nyscadv@nyscadv.org

North Carolina Coalition
Against Domestic Violence
115 Market Street, #400
Durham, NC 27701
(919) 956-9124
(888) 232-9124
www.nccadv.org

North Dakota Council
on Abused Women's
Services
418 E. Rosser Avenue,
#320
Bismark, ND 58501
(701) 255-6240
(888) 255-6240
 www.ndcaws.org
ndcaws@ndcaws.org

Ohio Domestic
Violence Network
4807 Evanswood Drive,
Suite 201
Columbus, Ohio 43229
614-781-9651
800-934-9840
www.odvn.org

info@odvn.org
Oklahoma Coalition
Against Domestic
Violence and Sexual
Assault
3815 N. Santa Fe Ave.,
Suite 124
Oklahoma City, OK 73118
(405) 524-0700
 www.ocadvsa.org

Oregon Coalition
Against Domestic
and Sexual Violence
380 SE Spokane
Street, #100
Portland, OR 97202
(503) 230-1951
 www.ocadsv.com

Pennsylvania Coalition
Against Domestic Violence
6400 Flank Drive, #1300
Harrisburg, PA 17112
(717) 545-6400
(800) 932-4632
 www.pcadv.org

The Office of Women
Advocates
P.O. Box 11382
Fernandez Juancus Station
Santurce, PR 00910
(787) 721-7676

Rhode Island Coalition
Against Domestic Violence
422 Post Road, #202
Warwick, RI 02888
(401) 467-9940
Fax (401) 467-9943
(800) 494-8100 In State
www.ricadv.org

South Carolina Coalition
Against Domestic Violence
and Sexual Assault
P.O. Box 7776
Columbia, SC 29202
(803) 256-2900
www.sccadvasa.org

South Dakota Coalition
Against Domestic Violence
& Sexual Assault
P.O. Box 141
Pierre, SD 57501
(605) 945-0869 or
(800) 572-9196
southdakotacoalition.org
sdcadvsa@rapidnet.com

Tennessee Coalition
Against
Domestic and Sexual
Violence
P.O. Box 120972
Nashville, TN 37212
(615) 386-9406 or
(800) 289-9018
www.tcadsv.org
Email: tcadsv@tcadsv.org

Texas Council on
Family Violence
P.O. Box 161810
Austin, TX 78716
(512) 794-1133 or
(800) 525-1978
www.tcfv.org

Women's Coalition
of St. Croix
Box 2734 (Christiansted)
St. Croix, VI 00822
(340) 773-9272
www.wcstx.com

Utah Domestic
Violence Council
205 North 400 West,
Salt Lake City, 84103
(801) 521-5544
www.udvac.org

Vermont Network Against
Domestic Violence and
Sexual Assault
P.O. Box 405
Montpelier, VT 05601
(802) 223-1302
www.vtnetwork.org
vtnetwork@vtnetwork.org

West Virginia Coalition
Against Domestic Violence
4710 Chimney Drive, #A
Charleston, WV 25302
(304) 965-3552
www.wvcadv.org

Virginians Against
Domestic Violence
2850 Sandy Bay Road,
#101
Williamsburg, VA 23185
(800) 838-8238
www.vadv.org
vadv@tni.net

Washington State Coalition
Against Domestic Violence
101 N. Capitol Way,
Olympia, WA 98501
(360) 586-1022
www.wscadv.org

Wyoming Coalition
Against Domestic
Violence and Sexual
Assault
409 South Fourth St.
Laramie, WY 82073
(800) 990-3877
www.wyomingdvsa.org

Wisconsin Coalition Against
Domestic Violence
307 S. Paterson Street, #1
Madison, WI 53703
(608) 255-0539
www.wcadv.org

SURVIVOR TIP INDEX

Cycle of Abuse

#1 The Honeymoon Phase: The abuser seduces and charms the victim. This is the stage where the victim "falls deeply in love" and often feels like they've known the abuser for much longer than they have.

#2 The Tension Phase: In this phase, early warning signs may appear but they are often dismissed as "little things." The abuser tries to control and isolate the victim from family and friends. Also, the victim tries not to make the abuser angry and tends to "walk on eggshells."

#3 The Explosion Phase: The abuser often makes physical threats, slaps or beats the victim in this phase. If the abuse is only emotional or verbal, it can still lead to physical abuse. The abuse will intensify and the frequency may increase, too.

Signs to Look for in Children

The major factor in protecting your child from abuse is identifying warning signs. It's critical to TRUST your INSTINCT. Here are red flags that indicate your child may be experiencing abuse:

- Frequent medical attention

- Genital bruising or bleeding

- Sexually transmitted diseases

- Inappropriate sexual behavior

- Fear of being left alone with people

- Fear of undressing

- Knowledge about sexual topics

- Nightmares

Sexual Assault Risks

Statistics show that over half of sexual assaults by known predators are not reported. Moreover, a sexual crime reported within 24 hours has a much greater chance of providing sufficient evidence for a conviction. But after 72 hours of the incident, the survivor is at a higher risk of losing DNA evidence. Reporting the crime within 24 hours helps to increase the chance of investigation, prosecution, and conviction.

Sexual assault survivors are:

- More likely to suffer from depression

- More likely to suffer from Post-Traumatic Stress Syndrome

- More likely to abuse alcohol or drugs

- More likely to attempt suicide

Abuse Prevention Tips for Churches

Religious organizations must take the proper steps to prevent inappropriate behavior and abuse. Here are some steps religious organizations can take:

- Vet leaders, volunteers and new hires with a more extensive application and screening process
- Require a criminal background check
- Require and check work and personal reference lists
- Establish a six-month rule before church staff or leaders can work with youth one-on-one
- Encourage the presence of both female and male chaperones or volunteers at church youth functions
- Establish clear rules about touching of minors
- Establish a buddy system with minors on church outings
- Discourage church leaders from facilitating one-on-one meetings in isolated environments

Workplace Tips

Title VII of the Civil Rights Act of 1964 deemed sexual harassment illegal as a form of gender discrimination. Here are five valuable tips you should know:

Tip #1: Document Everything. Be sure to keep a running file of dates, times and offensive incidents in question. Creating a verifiable track record of your complaints and the responses to them can be invaluable if you have to contest the problem, legally, or at work.

Tip #2: Don't Remain Silent. It's important to communicate that you find the perpetrator's conduct offensive and that it is creating tension. Perhaps the offender is unaware of bad behavior (such as jokes) and you may be able to resolve the problem. Remember, you are NOT powerless!

Tip #3: Detach from Bullying Behavior. Whatever you do, don't stoop to your offender's level and don't do or say anything that you may regret later. Losing your cool may create bigger problems along the way. Be smart about your reactions and the way you handle the harassment!

Tip #4: Know Your Employer's Procedure. Many companies have a documented procedure for handling sexual harassment claims. Ask your human resources representative for a copy of the employer's procedure, review it, and precisely follow the steps it outlines. If your company doesn't have a harassment procedure, make your supervisor or a higher-level manager aware of the problem.

Tip #5: Pursue Escalation. If you are unable to find resolution at your workplace, don't be afraid to contest the matter. Typically, the Equal Employment Opportunity Commission or your state's civil rights enforcement agency will investigate your claim and handle its resolution. If the agency is unable to resolve the matter but has deemed your claim valid, it will issue a "Right to Sue" letter. This letter will be valuable ammunition if you choose to file a civil lawsuit for injuries you suffered as a result of the bullying or harassment.

Stages of Grief

Stage 1: Denial is a defense mechanism that can occur when survivors are numb regarding their emotions. It is a temporary response to get the survivor through the initial pain they've experienced.

Stage 2: Anger helps survivors mask feelings of

denial and isolation. The anger in this stage is typically directed toward the person who caused them pain. It is sometimes directed toward anyone around the survivor.

Stage 3: Bargaining is the result of feelings of helplessness, guilt and vulnerability. These "if only" thoughts are another defense to accepting painful realities.

Stage 4: Depression is a stage of sadness and regret. The implications of the reality begin to set in as many survivors separate themselves from their loved ones. Comfort is a helpful remedy.

Stage 5: Acceptance is the final stage that not everyone experiences. It is not a stage of happiness, but rather a time of calm and withdrawal.

4 Ways to Support a Survivor

As mentioned earlier, your words, prayers, kind gestures, resources, and compassion can greatly assist a survivor with healing. If YOU are the survivor, then seeking professional help is likely the best form of self-care.

Some survivors say that a part of them died when they were abused. If you can relate to this analogy, you should also know that death is something that needs to be dealt with. Here are four methods to share comfort:

Offer a Listening Ear. Every survivor has a story or two to share. Offering a listening ear may inspire them to seek safety, get counseling, and avoid isolation. Just spending time out of your day to call them or meet them in person may play an important role in the healing process.

Validate Their Story. One of the most hurtful responses is when a survivor isn't believed. Or worse, when a survivor is blamed for the abuse. There is never an excuse to blame a victim. In addition, never respond to a survivor by saying, "I know how you feel," because each person's experience is unique. Simply respond by saying, "I'm here if you need me," or something of that nature.

Provide Resources. Asking a survivor what you can do to support them demonstrates love, and may help them avoid feeling of hopelessness. If you can't personally help them in any way, you can provide helpful contacts or direct them to where they can find much-needed resources.

Embrace Self-Care. Survivor stories can be traumatic, even for supporters. Listening to or supporting a survivor can be a long and draining process. There are times when it is appropriate to take a step back to avoid getting consumed by their hardships. Know when to embrace self-care in order to stay emotionally and psychologically healthy. This helps the survivor, because if you are mentally healthy you will be more motivated to show them support.

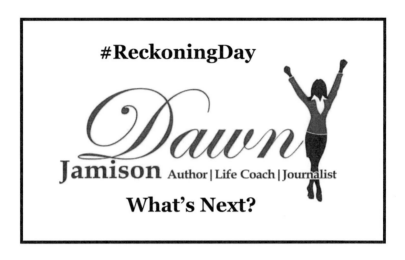

#ReckoningDay

Dawn

Jamison Author | Life Coach | Journalist

What's Next?

1. *Pretty* Please Give This Book a ★★★★★ Review!

If you are inspired by these stories, review my book on Amazon. Just search **"Reckoning Day"** and click on "Write a Customer Review."

2. Check out my other 2018 release,

The 8 Mistakes Women Make, at DawnJamison.com or buy it on Amazon. It's available on most book sites.

3. Let's stay connected! Visit DawnJamison.com to check out my "Living on Purpose" blog or

Get my Life Coaching tool called **"The Essential Happiness Plan"** in the areas of:

Confidence	Dating	Entrepreneurship
Spiritual	Marriage	Parenting
Career	Educational	

ABOUT THE AUTHOR

Born and raised in Grand Rapids, Mich., Dawn Jamison is a motivational author, certified life coach and journalist with 20 years of experience. She is co-founder of Quit for Passion, and president of The Renaissance Group. An avid international traveler and adventurer, Dawn can be found anywhere from climbing the Great Wall of China to discovering new exhibits at The Louvre Museum.

Dawn is a sought-after guest speaker for women's conferences, and is the author of *The 8 Mistakes Women Make*, and co-author of *The Female Leader Empowerment, Confidence & Passion*, and *The Women's Book of Empowerment & Confidence 365 Daily Affirmations*.

She is a graduate of the World Coaching Institute, and of Michigan State University and Aquinas College. She lives in the Motor City with her husband and daughter. She is happiest when she is motivating women to live their best lives.

DawnJamison.com
Facebook.com/ReckoningDay
Twitter: @IamDawnJamison
#ReckoningDay

COMING SOON: Available on eBook and Audiobook.